The New Handbook of Counseling Supervision

The classic edition of this groundbreaking book includes a new preface from the authors discussing developments in the field since the handbook's initial publication. Chapters provide an overview of best principles and best practices in counseling supervision process, one that is firmly rooted in the recent explosion of empirical research in this field.

Sponsored by the Association for Counselor Education and Supervision (ACES), the book is targeted primarily at master's-level practitioners who want practical, how-to applications of the research literature rather than a comprehensive review of the supervision literature. It's also a useful supplement for more academic texts used for doctoral-level instruction in counseling supervision.

L. DiAnne Borders, PhD, LMCHC, ACS, is Burlington Industries Excellence Professor in the counseling program at The University of North Carolina at Greensboro, where she teaches clinical supervision and supervises doctoral students' clinical supervision internships. She is the author of several books and numerous empirical and conceptual articles on clinical supervision. Her research is focused on novice supervisor development, supervision education and pedagogy, and process issues in clinical supervision, as well as trauma-informed supervision. She is editor of *The Clinical Supervisor*, the only international and interdisciplinary journal on supervision.

Lori L. Brown, PhD, is a professional school counselor in eastern North Carolina. She has worked as a counselor educator and clinical supervisor at several universities, and supervised practicing counselors in private supervision practice. Dr. Brown has written extensively on the topic of clinical supervision. She is a past president of the Southern Association of Counselor Education and Supervision and the Georgia Association of Counselor Education and Supervision.

Routledge Mental Health Classic Editions

The *Routledge Mental Health Classic Edition* series celebrates Routledge's commitment to excellence within the field of mental health. These books are recognized as timeless classics covering a range of important issues and continue to be recommended as key reading for professionals and students in the area. With a new introduction that explores what has changed since the books were first published, and why these books are as relevant now as ever, the series presents key ideas to a new generation.

Users and Abusers of Psychiatry
A Critical Look at Psychiatric Practice (Classic Edition)
By Lucy Johnstone

Psychotherapy: An Erotic Relationship
Transference and Countertransference Passions (Classic Edition)
By David Mann

Collective Trauma, Collective Healing
Promoting Community Resilience in the Aftermath of Disaster (Classic Edition)
By Jack Saul

Unlocking the Emotional Brain:
Eliminating Symptoms at Their Roots Using Memory Reconsolidation (Classic Edition)
By Bruce Ecker, Robin Ticic, and Laurel Hulley

The New Handbook of Counseling Supervision
(Classic Edition)
By L. DiAnne Borders and Lori L. Brown

For more information about this series, please visit: www.routledge.com

The New Handbook of Counseling Supervision

L. DiAnne Borders
Lori L. Brown

A product of the Association for Counselor Education and Supervision

Routledge
Taylor & Francis Group
NEW YORK AND LONDON

Cover image: © Nikada / Getty Images

Classic edition published 2022
by Routledge
605 Third Avenue, New York, NY 10158

and by Routledge
4 Park Square, Milton Park, Abingdon, Oxon, OX14 4RN

Routledge is an imprint of the Taylor & Francis Group, an informa business

First edition published by Routledge 2005

Library of Congress Cataloging-in-Publication Data
A catalog record for this book has been requested

ISBN: 978-1-032-17010-7 (hbk)
ISBN: 978-1-032-17008-4 (pbk)
ISBN: 978-1-003-25158-3 (ebk)

DOI: 10.4324/9781003251583

Typeset in Times New Roman
by Apex CoVantage, LLC

Contents

List of Tables

List of Appendices

Acknowledgments

Some 18 years ago, I set out—with much trepidation—to begin writing my part of what was to be a "brief brochure" on clinical supervision. This work was done at the invitation of Dr. Nancy Scott, who, as 1986–1987 President of the Association for Counselor Education and Supervision (ACES), had chosen "Spectrum on Supervision" as her theme. Nancy's goal was to address the lack of supervision training materials by providing a basic and accessible guideline for supervision practice. I was a relatively new assistant professor in my first counselor educator position at Oakland University, and a new cochair, with George Leddick, of the ACES Supervision Interest Network. George and I were selected as authors due to our Network positions. Fairly quickly, we realized that we had more than a brief brochure, and Nancy and ACES gave us the go-ahead to write a monograph-length book instead. My memories of those hours at my desk include many moments of doubt and questioning. "I don't know how to write a book!" I often thought, along with "I don't have enough supervision experience to be doing this!" Both George and Nancy, as well as other ACES members, waved away such talk, made helpful suggestions, and provided much encouragement. I don't think any of us, however, thought sales of the *Handbook of Counseling Supervision* would survive the first printing.

In working on this *New Handbook*, I have often remembered that initial conversation with Nancy Scott with some amazement and much appreciation. Similarly, over the years since publication of the first *Handbook*, a number of ACES colleagues have provided instructive guidance and steadfast support for a number of other ACES-sponsored Supervision Network projects (i.e., the Standards for Counseling Supervisors, Curriculum Guide for Training Counseling Supervisors, and Ethical Guidelines for Counseling Supervisors; see Appendices A, B, and C, this volume), each of which was a new, first-time experience for me. Similarly, ACES leaders' interest in an update of the *Handbook*, particularly Fred Bradley's persistent urgings, was instrumental in making this new book a possibility. I am grateful to have this opportunity to thank my ACES colleagues for providing me with so many professional opportunities over the years, as well as the patience, encouragement, belief, and feedback that helped the opportunities become completed projects. It also should be said that "there's a lot of Peggy Fong" here, as much of what I know and believe about supervision was gleaned from my time as Peggy's student, supervisee, mentee, and colleague.

Finally, I want to acknowledge the powerful learning experiences provided by my supervisees at the University of Florida, Oakland University, and the University of North Carolina at Greensboro (UNCG), including the UNCG doctoral students who have expanded my perspectives through their supervised supervision experiences, dissertation research, and dialogues. Several have gone on to establish their own areas of supervision research expertise, while others have shared delightful stories of their supervision practice experiences. One is coauthor of this *New Handbook*. My learnings from these students, former students, and other supervisees are infused throughout this book, with much appreciation.

—L. DiAnne Borders

I must admit that when my coauthor, Dr. L. DiAnne Borders, invited me to be a part of this revised handbook, I was simply overcome. How did she decide to ask me? Did I really know enough about supervision to be writing about it in such an important document? Could I do this? Then I started thinking back over my years of learning about (and from) supervision, and realized that this topic has been my main professional interest for more than 10 years now. I was interested in counseling supervision before I started my doctoral program at UNCG and met DiAnne, but once I started talking to and learning from her about the topic, I found my passion. DiAnne has been my teacher, my supervisor, my dissertation chair, my colleague, and my mentor. Without her, I would never have come this far.

My school counseling master's internship supervisor, Dr. Pamela O. Paisley, awakened me to the fantastic benefits of supervision. Pam has also served as a mentor throughout my professional career, and for her support and friendship I am eternally grateful. As doctoral students at UNCG, my friends and colleagues learned about supervision along with me, and helped me learn, as well. Dr. Michael T. Garrett (Western Carolina University) and Dr. Sondra Smith Adcock (University of Florida) continue to inspire me to be the best counseling supervisor I can be. During my early years as a Counselor Educator, my colleagues at Columbus State University, Dr. Michael L. Baltimore, Dr. S. Lenoir Gillam, Dr. Marty J. Jencius (Kent State University), and Dr. Robin Wilbourn Lee (University of Tennessee, Chattanooga), helped me continue to learn about what it takes to be a good supervisor. Although some of us moved on to other positions, to this day these are the colleagues I contact first when I need to consult about my own supervisory skills.

And last of all, I would be remiss if I did not acknowledge the practitioners and students I have supervised over the years. Those practicing school counselors in northwestern North Carolina who participated in my dissertation study on counseling supervision taught me just how important it was to promote counseling supervision opportunities for professional school counselors. My student supervisees at Columbus State University and Clemson University provided me with amazing opportunities for self-reflection and growth as a supervisor. The professional school counselors I worked with as part of my private supervision practice in Columbus, GA, allowed me to see the beauty and importance of providing counseling supervision for practitioners. To all of you, I express my appreciation and continued thanks for teaching me so much and so well.

—Lori L. Brown

We express our collective thanks to our reviewers, who provided instructive and helpful feedback: Dr. Michael Baltimore, Columbus State University; Dr. Catharina Chang, Georgia State University; Dr. James Korcuska, University of South Dakota at Vermillion; and Dr. Cynthia Osborn, Kent State University. Finally, we offer our appreciation to Dr. David Zimpfer (ACES) for his guidance and assistance through the publication process.

—LDB and LLB

Preface to the Classic Edition

I (LDB) started compiling a bibliography of clinical supervision publications in the 1990s. I wanted students in my first doctoral-level supervision course to see the range of topics they might choose from for their course project. Over the years, that bibliography has ballooned to 150 pages, (single spaced, 10 pt. type), and it in no way begins to cover all the books, chapters, journal articles, and media focused on some aspect of clinical supervision.

Indeed, recognition of clinical supervision as the *signature pedagogy* – in multiple professions – has exploded globally and across a range of disciplines since publication of *The New Handbook of Counseling Supervision* some 15 years ago. This surge is evident in a range of health-related professions (e.g., counseling, social work, psychology, medicine and nursing, speech-language pathology and audiology, corrections), and beyond (e.g., sports coaching), around the world. The by-products are many.

For example, within mental health specifically, professional groups have promulgated supervision competencies (e.g., American Board of Examiners in Clinical Social Work, 2004; Falender et al., 2004; Gonsalvez & Milne, 2010; Roth & Pilling, 2008) and best practices for supervision practice and training (e.g., Borders et al., 2014; National Association of Social Workers & Association of Social Work Boards, 2013), with similar advocacy ongoing in several countries (e.g., Turkey, counseling, Aladag & Kemer, 2016; Ireland, counseling psychology, Creaner & Timlak, 2016; South Africa, social work, Engelbrecht, 2019; see also Watkins & Milne, 2014). There is an international credential (Approved Clinical Supervisor, https://www.cce-global.org/credentialing/acs) and, in the US, a number of state-level licenses for supervision practice (see Borders et al., 2014). International and interdisciplinary developments include the growth of a journal (*The Clinical Supervisor*, https://www.tandfonline.com/loi/wcsu20) and conference specific to clinical supervision (http://iiccs2021.catholic.edu/), as well as the launch of the Clinical Supervision Research Collaborative at the 2020 conference. In at least three countries (Australia and United Kingdom, psychologists; New Zealand, social workers), ongoing supervision across a clinician's professional lifespan is now the norm for certain disciplines.

In addition, a wealth of new publications, especially empirical research, has both broadened and deepened our knowledge of supervision practice. Researchers have documented the impact of active learning strategies (e.g., Bearman et al., 2013) and the importance of direct observation of supervisees' work (McMahon & Ledden, 2019; North, 2013). They have created a number of new supervision measures (e.g., Calvert et al., 2020; Fukui et al., 2014; Li et al., 2020; White & Winstanley, 2010; see also Tangen & Borders, 2016) and worked to improve assessment and evaluation of supervisees (e.g., Cleak et al., 2015; Gonsalvez et al., 2017; Wilkins et al., 2018). A few have put the spotlight on client (e.g., Cook et al., 2019; Grossl et al., 2014; Milne, 2014) and patient (e.g., Farnan et al., 2012) outcomes, the newest (and shortest) section on LDB's supervision bibliography.

At the same time, however, fundamental truths about clinical supervision have been reinforced repeatedly. The prevailing relevance of foundational models from the 1980s – Bernard's (1979) discrimination matrix and developmental descriptions of supervisee growth (e.g., Skovholt & Ronnestad, 1992; Stoltenberg & Delworth, 1987) – have continued to inform supervision in new arenas. The most fundamental truth – the central, pivotal role of the supervisory relationship for every other aspect of the clinical supervision enterprise – has been asserted over and over. Such truths were the bedrock of *The New Handbook of Counseling Supervision*, and thus underscore the book's continued relevance in the 2020s. We are aware, for example, that it is a text for academic courses for master's and doctoral students as well as professional development for practitioners (online and face-to-face) in the US and abroad. It is worth restating that "the principles underlying effective supervision are basic, but they become very complex in practice" (Borders & Brown, 2005, p. xiv).

What has changed is expanded awareness of that complexity, the multiple layers at play in supervision practice. In particular, researchers have uncovered many intricacies that can define a *safe* supervisory relationship, based on characteristics of the supervisee (e.g., attachment, intersecting identities) as well as their clients (e.g., trauma history). Safety is clearly relevant to supervisee nondisclosure (e.g., Cook & Welfare, 2018), relationship ruptures – and their repair – (e.g., Friedlander, 2015), as well as a startling number of occurrences of harmful supervision (e.g., Ellis et al., 2017). Researchers have explored the multifaceted dynamics of corrective feedback (e.g., Borders et al., 2017; Hoffman et al., 2005) and other "courageous conversations" (Davys, 2019).

Safety factors have been particularly enriched by findings from explorations of cultural dynamics within the supervisory relationship. Researchers have documented the negative impact of microaggressions (e.g., Constantine & Sue, 2007; Pieterse, 2018) and the positive effects of broaching identities (e.g., Jones et al., 2019), as well as the challenges inherent in cross-racial supervisory dyads (e.g., Burkard et al., 2014). Others have called attention to a need to broaden attention on multicultural competencies to embrace cultural humility (e.g., Watkins et al., 2019). Some have highlighted supervisors' responsibilities to model and teach social justice (e.g., Asakura & Maurer, 2018; Chang et al., 2010; Dollarhide et al., 2021).

This brief, and selected, summary highlights some of the supervision advances and insights gained over the last 15 years. A nagging question for us, however, is to what extent all this new knowledge has trickled out to supervisors in the field – or perhaps even reflects the questions most salient to them. Unfortunately, the research-practice gap is still alive in clinical supervision. In response, there are increasing calls for researchers to peer inside the actual practice of supervision in action (e.g., Goodyear et al., 2016), what Ladany et al. (2005) described as "the kind of knowledge that practitioners need for their actual, day-to-day work with supervisees" …, the "how and under what conditions" (p. 5). Hopefully, over the next 15 years, researchers will heed calls to employ methodologies (e.g., case studies; Goodyear et al., 2016) and data collection approaches (e.g., Interpersonal Process Recall, Grant et al., 2012) that can shed light on the realities of supervisors' work – their ongoing thoughts, decisions, and choices during a session.

We need to better understand the messiness involved in prioritizing the multiple, sometimes conflicting, needs of the supervisee and client. We need to chronicle how supervisors fumble, and recover, in response to the intriguing nuances and ambiguities in front of them. How, despite confusion and doubts, supervisors work to act in good faith and in line with their ethical mandates. Such findings not only would greatly inform supervision practice. They also would be instructive for supervision training, of both doctoral students and practitioners in the field, as well as what post-training opportunities (e.g., supervision of supervision, consultation) would best support their continued professional development. Indeed, the pedagogical underpinnings of the signature pedagogy of so many professions are still relatively unexplored (Borders, 2019; Goodyear, 2014; McLeod et al., 2003).

We are honored by the re-issue of the *Handbook* as part of Routledge's classic series, a decision that seems to reinforce the fundamental truths presented in the book. Based on recent research, our own experience, and anecdotes shared with us by other supervision educators, we believe the *Handbook* still provides the necessary basics for new supervisors to get started on the right foot. Given its practical application, still grounded in research and reflecting best practices, the *Handbook* provides initial responses to the 'how to' and 'what does that look like' questions new supervisors inevitably ask. At the same time, we still view the *Handbook* as a "Clinical Supervision 101" text which should be supplemented by other readings – and active learning experiences – specific to the training context as well as the supervision practice setting, population, discipline, country, and culture.

Thus, we hope readers of the *Handbook* not only will be informed, but also encouraged to read further, and consult often, around the issues and challenges that perplex and fascinate them as they navigate their own supervision adventure. Along the way, we hope many will report their discoveries, adding their own contributions to our evolving understanding of the dynamic power of clinical supervision. Such ongoing work will surely benefit supervisors and supervisees, as well as their clients.

L. DiAnne Borders and Lori L. Brown
January 2021

References

Aladag, M., & Kemer, G. (2016). Clinical supervision: An emerging counseling specialty in Turkey [Global Developments in Clinical Supervision series]. *The Clinical Supervisor, 35*(2), 175–191.

American Board of Examiners in Clinical Social Work. (2004, October). *Clinical supervision: A practice specialty of clinical social work.* Author.

Asakura, K., & Maurer, K. (2018). Attending to social justice in clinical social work: Supervision as a pedagogical space. *Clinical Social Work Journal, 46*(4), 289–297.

Association for Counselor Education and Supervision. (2011). *Best practices in clinical supervision.* Alexandria, VA: Author. Retrieved from http://www.acesonline.net/wpcontent/uploads./2011/10/ACES-Best-Practices-in-clinical-supervison-document-FINAL.pdf

Bearman, S. K., Weisz, J. R., Chorpita, B. F., Hoagwood, K., Ward, A., Ugueto, A. M., & Bernstein, A. (2013). More practice, less preach? The role of supervision processes and therapist characteristics in EBP implementation. *Administration and Policy in Mental Health and Mental Health Services Research, 40*(6), 518–529.

Bernard, J. M. (1979). Supervisory training: A discrimination model. *Counselor Education and Supervision, 19*(1), 60–68.

Borders, L. D. (2019). Science of Learning: Evidence-based teaching in the clinical supervision classroom. *Counselor Education and Supervision, 58*(1), 64–69.

Borders, L. D., Glosoff, H. L., Welfare, L. E., Hays, D. G., DeKruyf, L., Fernando, D. M., & Page, B. (2014). Best Practices in Clinical Supervision: Evolution of a counseling specialty. *The Clinical Supervisor, 33*(1), 26–44.

Borders, L. D., Welfare, L. E., Sackett, C. R., & Cashwell, C. S. (2017). New supervisors' struggles and successes with corrective feedback. *Counselor Education and Supervision, 56*(3), 208–224.

Burkard, A. W., Knox, S., Clarke, R. D., Phelps, D. L., & Inman, A. G. (2014). Supervisors' experiences of providing difficult feedback in cross-ethnic/racial supervision. *The Counseling Psychologist, 42*(3), 314–344.

Calvert, F. L., Deane, F. P., & Brin, F. S. G. (2020). Supervisee perceptions of the use of metacommunication in the supervisory relationship. *Psychotherapy Research, 30*(2), 228–238.

Chang, C. Y., Crethar, H. C., & Ratts, M. J. (2010). Social justice: A national imperative for counselor education and supervision [Special issue]. *Counselor Education and Supervision, 50*(2).

Cleak, H., Hawkins, L., Laughton, J., & Williams, J. (2015). Creating a standardised teaching and learning framework for social work field placements. *Australian Social Work, 68*(1), 49–64. https://doi.org/10.1080/0312407X.2014.932401

Constantine, M. G., & Sue, D. W. (2007). Perceptions of racial microaggressions among Black supervisees in cross-racial dyads. *Journal of Counseling Psychology, 54*(2), 142–153.

Cook, A. L., Brodsky, L., Gracia, R., & Morizio, L. J. (2019). Exploring multicultural and social justice counseling training outcomes on school counselor and youth development. *Counseling Outcome Research and Evaluation, 10*(2), 78–93.

Cook, R. M., & Welfare, L. E. (2018). Examining predictors of counselor-in-training intentional nondisclosure. *Counselor Education and Supervision, 57*(3), 211–226.

Creaner, M., & Timulak, L. (2016). Clinical supervision and counseling psychology in the Republic of Ireland [Global Development in Clinical Supervision series]. *The Clinical Supervisor, 35*(2), 192–209.

Davys, A. (2019). Courageous conversations in supervision. *Aotearoa New Zealand Social Work, 31*(3), 78–86.

Dollarhide, C. T., Hale, S. C., & Stone-Sabali, S. (2021). A new model for social justice supervision. *Journal of Counseling & Development, 99*(1), 104–113.

Ellis, M. V., Corp, D. A., Taylor, E. J., & Kangos, K. A. (2017). Narratives of harmful clinical supervision: An unacknowledged truth [Special issue]. *The Clinical Supervisor, 36*(1).

Engelbrecht, L. K. (2019). Towards authentic supervision of social workers in South Africa [Global Developments in Clinical Supervision Series]. *The Clinical Supervisor, 38*(2), 301–325.

Falender, C. A., Comish, J. A., Goodyear, R., Hatcher, R., Kaslow, N. J., Leventhal, G., et al. (2004). Defining competencies in psychology supervision: A consensus statement. *Journal of Clinical Psychology, 60*(7), 771–787.

Farnan, J. M., Petty, L. A., Georgitis, E., Martin, Sh., Chiu, E., Prochaska, M., & Arora, V. M. (2012). The effect of clinical supervision on patient and residency education outcomes. *Academic Medicine, 87*(4), 428–442.

Fukui, S., Rapp, C. A., Goscha, R., Marty, D., & Ezell, M. (2014). The Perceptions of Supervisory Support Scale. *Administration and Policy in Mental Health and Mental Health Services Research, 41*(3), 353–359. https://doi.org/10.1007/s10488-013-0470-z

Friedlander, M. L. (2015). Use of relational strategies to repair alliance ruptures: How responsive supervisors train responsive psychotherapists. *Psychotherapy, 52*(2), 174–179.

Gonsalvez, C. J., & Milne, D. L. (2010). Clinical supervisor training in Australia: A review of current problems and possible solutions. *Australian Psychologist, 45*(4), 233–242.

Gonsalvez, C. J., Wahnon, T., & Deane, F. P. (2017). Goal setting, feedback, and assessment practices reported by Australian clinical supervisors. *Australian Psychologist, 52*(1), 21–30.

Goodyear, R. K. (2014). Supervision as pedagogy: Attending to its essential instructional and learning processes. *The Clinical Supervisor, 33*(1), 82–99.

Goodyear, R. K., Borders, L. D., Chang, C. Y., Guiffrida, D. A., Hutman, H., Kemer, G., Watkins, C. E., Jr., & White, E. (2016). Prioritizing questions and methods for an international and interdisciplinary supervision research agenda: Suggestions by eight scholars. *The Clinical Supervisor 35*(1), 117–154.

Grant, J., Schofield, M. J., & Crawford, S. (2012). Managing difficulties in supervision: Supervisors' perspectives. *Journal of Counseling Psychology, 59*(4), 528–541.

Grossl, A. B., Reese, R. J., Norsworthy, L. A., & Hopkins, N. B. (2014). Client feedback data in supervision: Effects on supervision and outcome. *Training and Education in Professional Psychology, 8*(3), 182–188.

Hoffman, M. A., Hill, C. E., Holmes, S. E., & Freitas, G. F. (2005). Supervisor perspective on the process and outcome of giving easy, difficult, or no feedback to supervisees. *Journal of Counseling Psychology, 52*(1), 3–13.

Jones, C. T., Welfare, L. E., Melchior, S., & Cash, R. M. (2019). Broaching as a strategy for intercultural understanding in clinical supervision. *The Clinical Supervisor, 38*(1), 1–16.

Ladany, N., Friedlander, M. L., & Nelson, M. L. (2005). *Critical incidents in supervision.* American Psychological Association.

Li, C., Kemer, G., & Henson, J. M. (2020). Development and validation of the Supervisee Disclosure in Supervision Scale. *Counselor Education and Supervision, 59*(2), 145–159.

McLeod, P. J, Steinert, Y., Meagher, T., & McLeod, A. (2003). The ABCs of pedagogy for clinical teachers. *Medical Education, 37*(7), 638–644.

McMahon, A., & Ledden, K. (2018). Recording client sessions during psychotherapy training: From "an absurd idea" to "potent learning." *Counselling & Psychotherapy Research, 19*(3), 241–251.

Milne, D. (2014). Beyond the "acid test": A conceptual review and reformulation of outcome evaluation in clinical supervision. *American Journal of Psychotherapy, 68*(2), 213–230.

National Association of Social Workers & Association of Social Work Boards. (2013). *Best practice standards in social work supervision.* Authors. https://www.socialworkers.org/LinkClick.aspx?fileticket=GBrLbl4BuwI%3D&portalid=0

North, G. J. (2013). Recording supervision: Educational, therapeutic, and enhances the supervisory working alliance? *Psychotherapy Research, 13*(1), 61–70.

Pieterse, A. L. (2018). Attending to racial trauma in clinical supervision: Enhancing client and supervisee outcomes. *The Clinical Supervisor, 37*(1), 204–220.

Roth, A., & Pilling, S. (2008). *A competence framework for the supervision of psychological therapies.* Retrieved June 30, 2013, from http://www.ucl.ac.uk/clinical-psychology/CORE/supervision_framework.

Skovolt, T. M., & Rønnestad, M. H. (1992). Themes in therapist and counselor development. *Journal of Counseling & Development, 70*(4), 505–515.

Stoltenberg, C. D., & Delworth, U. (1987). *Supervising counselors and therapists: A developmental approach.* Jossey-Bass.

Tangen, J. L., & Borders, L. D. (2016). The supervisory relationship: A conceptual and psychometric review of measures. *Counselor Education and Supervision, 55*(3), 159–181.

Watkins, C. E., Jr., Hook, J. N., Owen, J., DeBlaere, C., Davis, D. E., & Von Tongeren, D. R. (2019). Multicultural orientation in psychotherapy supervision: Cultural humility, cultural comfort, and cultural opportunities. *American Journal of Psychotherapy, 72*(2), 38–46.

Watkins, C. E., Jr., & Milne, D. (Eds.). (2014). *Wiley International Handbook of Clinical Supervision.* Oxford, UK: Wiley.

White, E., & Winstanley, J. (2010). A randomized controlled trial of clinical supervision: Selected findings from a novel Australian attempt to establish the evidence base for causal relationships with quality of care and patient outcomes, as an informed contribution to mental health nursing practice development. *Journal of Research in Nursing, 15*(2), 151–167.

Wilkins, D., Khan, M., Stabler, L., Newlands, F., & Mcdonnell, J. (2018). Evaluating the quality of social work supervision in UK children's services: Comparing self-report and independent observations. *Clinical Social Work Journal*, *46*(4), 350–360. https://doi.org/10.1007/s10615-018-0680-7

Preface to the First Edition

When the original *Handbook of Counseling Supervision* (Borders & Leddick, 1987) was published in 1987, it was the first and only book of its kind. More than 15 years later, the *Handbook* enjoys the company of several comprehensive textbooks (most notably, Bernard & Goodyear's, 1992, 1998, 2004, *Fundamentals of Clinical Supervision*) and several other monographs and books that summarize a particular line of research (e.g., Holloway, 1995) or a particular training approach (e.g., Neufeldt, Iversen, & Juntunen, 1995), cover one aspect of the supervision process, such as legal issues (e.g., Disney & Stephens, 1994), or offer a very applied workbook. Clearly, leadership of the Association for Counselor Education and Supervision (ACES) in 1986–1987 correctly gauged the need for a practice-oriented publication on counseling supervision. Just as clearly, much has happened in the field since that publication.

The *Handbook,* however, continues to be a unique publication. It was designed to bridge theory, research, and practice—to translate academic knowledge into best practices, for use in training programs for master's level and doctoral level practitioners. This "niche" still exists. In fact, it has expanded. During the past few years there has been a proliferation of continuing education training programs in counseling supervision, and a growing awareness among practitioners, across helping professions, of the need for specialized training. In addition, almost all counselor education doctoral programs require a course in counseling supervision.

Thus, the New Handbook is written within the same framework as the original—a "best principles" and "best practices" overview of the counseling supervision process that is firmly based in current literature, particularly the explosion of empirical research on supervision published over the past few decades. Readers will not find a comprehensive review of the supervision literature. This is best covered—and has been covered—in journal articles and textbooks. Here, the focus is on application of current knowledge gleaned from the supervision literature, based in our own research, our ongoing study of the literature, and our efforts to translate results for our students and workshop participants. As in the original, the presentation is targeted primarily at master's level practitioners, a sophisticated group who, in our experience, prefer "how to" explanations with examples. At the same time, we believe this revision also will serve as a useful supplement for more academic texts used for doctoral-level instruction in counseling supervision.

It has been our experience that the principles underlying effective supervision are basic, but they become very complex in practice. Here, we have attempted to present, explain, and illustrate these complexities—the fascinating nuances that truly inform effective practice. In addition, in light of evolutions in the field, expanded attention has been given to multicultural and diversity issues, and chapters on group supervision and technology have been added. Also new are discussion questions and vignettes meant to enhance application of key concepts in each chapter. We also have added more sample materials and forms for practice. In short, this is not a revision, but truly a *New Handbook.*

Supervision has been a fascinating experience for us for some years, from our earliest experiences as nervous but eager supervisees, to our first attempts to provide instructive and supportive supervision, to our efforts to address the crying need for supervision training resources. We hope that, wherever you are along this continuum of supervision-related experience, the *New Handbook* provides some helpful direction.

—L. DiAnne Borders and
—Lori L. Brown

Chapter 1

Supervision Models and Principles

All readers, regardless of their experience as a supervisor, come to the *New Handbook of Counseling Supervision* with a good bit of knowledge about the supervision process. Those of you who have been in the role of supervisee only still have ideas and opinions regarding what works and how you would "do supervision." Chances are likely that you are right about many of your ideas. Those of you who have extensive supervision experience, whether trained as a supervisor or not, at the least have some practice-based observations and conclusions that probably can be found in the supervision literature. Quite simply, even untrained supervisors arrive at their first supervision session with a good bit of relevant training and experience. Certainly, all arrive with extensive training as a counselor, and everything learned in one's master's or doctoral program in counseling is relevant to supervision. Every Council for Accreditation of Counseling and Related Education Programs (CACREP) area addressed in our counselor education accreditation standards (CACREP, 2001)—counseling theories, assessment devices, helping and consulting skills, change interventions, ethical and legal guidelines, lifespan development and career development theories, family and group dynamics, social and cultural foundations, research and evaluation—has obvious application to helping a supervisee better understand and work with a client. Less obvious is the application of one's counseling background for better understanding of and working with a supervisee. However, as a trained counselor, you know how to establish rapport and create a working relationship with your supervisee, you understand the implications of a supervisee's life stage to his or her approach to clients, and you are aware of the varied influences (e.g., family history, ethnicity, and gender) on your supervisee's behavior. Your knowledge of change mechanisms, including motivations toward and resistance to change, also are relevant to a supervisee's growth as a professional counselor. Both your empathic and your confrontive skills will be needed.

Those of you who have some teaching experience bring other relevant knowledge and skills to the supervision context, including your background in learning theories and instructional strategies. You know how to establish both short-term *lesson* plan objectives (a supervision session) and long-term

DOI: 10.4324/9781003251583-1

unit plan goals (semester), and have experience in designing evaluations of progress. You understand the importance of flexibility in teaching strategies to address a variety of learning styles as well as the use of complementary strategies (e.g., didactic and experiential) and active learning approaches to consolidate learning. You have practice breaking down feedback into manageable chunks, concrete suggestions, and sequential steps.

Other professional backgrounds also have relevance for your work as a counseling supervisor. From consultation training, one has additional assessment and facilitation skills. From research courses, one understands the importance of ongoing evaluation of one's work, as well as the skills for stating testable hypotheses, gathering relevant data from multiple sources, maintaining objectivity, and appropriately limiting the generalizability of your results to other supervisees. In fact, we have seen supervisors draw from their experiences in a wide array of professional experiences, including business (e.g., establishing a contract), computer and information systems (e.g., comfort using technology), dance (e.g., a fine sensitivity to body movements), engineering (e.g., ordering all the parts into a system), and theology (e.g., the relevance of grace and deep understanding of moral values underlying ethical decision making).

Clearly, the point here is that all new supervisors already have knowledge and skills highly applicable to their work as a supervisor. Why, then, is supervisor training needed? First, knowledge and skills from other professional areas are used in new and unique ways in supervision. You will use your counseling skills, but you will not be a counselor for your supervisee. You will use your teaching skills but will apply them in a specialized, nonclassroom setting, within an ongoing relationship. Part of supervision training, then, is learning how to apply existing skills appropriately in supervision. Second, it is quite important to have a framework for conducting supervision, a schema for organizing one's knowledge and skills and deciding when and how to use them. Third, there are some interventions, learning processes, and ethical and legal considerations unique to supervision, and these need to be learned during supervisor training. Supervision, then, truly is a unique, separate profession (Dye & Borders, 1990).

As an initial step in your supervisor training, then, we suggest you first take an inventory of the relevant knowledge and skills you bring to your new role as a supervisor. There are several tools for doing this, including a self-assessment resumé in Borders and Leddick (1987), reprinted here (see Tables 1.1, 1.2, and 1.3). Similarly, the Association for Counselor Education and Supervision (ACES) Standards for Counseling Supervisors (Dye & Borders, 1990) provide an overview of 11 core areas of knowledge, competence, and personal traits that can be used as a self-assessment checklist (see Appendix A). These standards are operationalized in the ACES Curriculum Guide for Training Counseling Supervisors (Borders et al., 1991; see Appendix B). These tools will help you get a quick overview of what you need to know to be an effective supervisor, as well as what you already know, and which areas require focused work.

Table 1.1 Resumé Format for a Self-Assessment of Knowledge and Skills Developed in Previous Supervision-Related Roles and Experiences

Supervision-Related Roles, Skills, and Knowledge

Name______________________	Date__________________________
Teacher Role Date	Position, setting, clients Descriptive statement of knowledge and skills
Counselor Role Date	Position, setting, clients Descriptive statement of knowledge and skills
Consultant Role Date	Position, setting, clients Descriptive statement of knowledge and skills
Researcher Role Date	Descriptive statement of knowledge and skills
Supervisor Role Date	Position, setting, supervisees Descriptive statement of knowledge and skills
Supervisee Role	
Setting	Supervisor

Date
- Mode of supervision
- Individual and/or group
- Interventions (e.g., audiotapes, IPR, casenotes)
- Supervisor's counseling orientation
- Supervisor's supervision style, including relationship/interpersonal

Reprinted from Borders, L. D., & Leddick, G. R. (1987). *Handbook of counseling supervision* (p. 8). Alexandria, VA: Association for Counselor Education and Supervision.

Table 1.2 Self-Assessment of Supervision-Related Knowledge and Skills

Teaching skills	*Needs Development*				*Expertise*
Ability to identify learning needs of supervisee	1	2	3	4	5
Ability to identify learning style of supervisee	1	2	3	4	5
Ability to write learning goals and objectives	1	2	3	4	5
Ability to devise instructional strategies to accommodate needs and learning style of supervisee	1	2	3	4	5
Ability to present material in a didactic manner	1	2	3	4	5
Ability to present material in an experiential manner (e.g., demonstrate, model)	1	2	3	4	5
Ability to explain the rationale for an intervention	1	2	3	4	5
Ability to evaluate supervisee's learning	1	2	3	4	5
Comfort in authority role	1	2	3	4	5
Ability to give constructive feedback to supervisee	1	2	3	4	5
Other ____________________________	1	2	3	4	5

(*Continued*)

Table 1.2 (Continued)

Teaching skills	*Needs Development*				*Expertise*
Counseling skills					
Ability to establish rapport, a working relationship with supervisee	1	2	3	4	5
Facilitative skills (e.g., warmth, primary empathy, genuineness, concreteness, etc.)	1	2	3	4	5
Challenging skills (e.g., self-disclosure, advanced empathy, confrontation, immediacy, etc.)	1	2	3	4	5
Ability to facilitate supervisee self-exploration of strengths, limitations, and concerns about counseling skills	1	2	3	4	5
Ability to help supervisee explore feelings about client, purposes of counseling, counseling interventions	1	2	3	4	5
Ability to help supervisee explore feelings about supervision	1	2	3	4	5
Ability to conduct intake sessions	1	2	3	4	5
Ability to conduct closure sessions	1	2	3	4	5
Ability to make referrals	1	2	3	4	5
Knowledge of interpersonal dynamics	1	2	3	4	5
Knowledge of counseling theories	1	2	3	4	5
Expertise in counseling techniques (specify)	1	2	3	4	5
Expertise with particular clients and issues (e.g., suicide, career)	1	2	3	4	5
Ability to identify themes, patterns of behavior	1	2	3	4	5
Ability to handle counseling skills	1	2	3	4	5
Ability to respond with flexibility	1	2	3	4	5
Ability to integrate data about supervisee into comprehensive "case conceptualization"	1	2	3	4	5
Other ______________________________	1	2	3	4	5

Consultation skills	*Needs Development*				*Expertise*
Ability to objectively assess problem situation	1	2	3	4	5
Ability to provide alternative interventions and/or conceptualization or problem/client	1	2	3	4	5
Ability to facilitate supervisee brainstorming of alternatives, options, solutions	1	2	3	4	5
Ability to encourage supervisee to make own choices, take responsibility for decisions concerning client and counseling	1	2	3	4	5
Ability to function in more peer-like, collegial relationship with supervisee	1	2	3	4	5
Other ______________________________	1	2	3	4	5

Consultation skills	*Needs Development*				*Expertise*
Research skills					
Ability to make accurate and reliable observations (of client and of supervisee)	1	2	3	4	5
Ability to state testable hypothesis (e.g., Is supervisee avoiding confrontation? Would role-playing be an effective supervision intervention?)	1	2	3	4	5
Ability to gather data relevant to testing hypothesis	1	2	3	4	5
Ability to evaluate hypothesis	1	2	3	4	5
Ability to incorporate new data, restate and retest hypothesis	1	2	3	4	5
Ability to identify confounding variables affecting change (e.g., supervisees' personal issues)	1	2	3	4	5
Ability to critically examine and incorporate new research into supervision (e.g., on counselor–client dynamics, assessment, counseling intervention, supervision intervention)	1	2	3	4	5
Other ______________________	1	2	3	4	5

Reprinted from Borders, L. D., & Leddick, G. R. (1987). *Handbook of counseling supervision* (pp. 9–10). Alexandria, VA: Association for Counselor Education and Supervision.

As part of your self-inventory, give particular emphasis to feedback you have received about your work as a counselor, teacher, consultant, and other positions. If you are reluctant to use confrontation skills in counseling, this likely will be true of you in supervision also. If you used experiential activities effectively in the classroom, this will be a strength you can draw on during supervision. Review of feedback about your previous work provides a solid foundation for creating individual goals for your supervisor training experience.

We do offer one word of caution about drawing from your previous experiences, particularly as a supervisee. What worked for you within any particular supervisory relationship should not be overgeneralized as "the right way." What worked in that supervision context was influenced by the personalities of the supervisor and supervisee as well as their race and gender, the supervisee's developmental level, the culture of the setting, types of client issues, and many other variables. Indeed, although we present a number of principles and dynamics underlying the supervision process, these principles and dynamics play out in unique ways within each supervision experience. These

Table 1.3 Self-Assessment of Supervision-Related Abilities Developed as a Supervisee

	Needs Development			*Expertise*	
Ability to evaluate audiotapes and videotapes	1	2	3	4	5
Ability to write case notes	1	2	3	4	5
Ability to identify strengths and areas for improvement	1	2	3	4	5
Ability to relate to supervisor	1	2	3	4	5
Ability to communicate needs to supervisor	1	2	3	4	5
Ability to plan and make case presentation	1	2	3	4	5
Ability to receive feedback	1	2	3	4	5
Willingness to be self-critical	1	2	3	4	5
Other ______________________	1	2	3	4	5
As peer supervisor					
Ability to conceptualize case based on peer counselor's presentation	1	2	3	4	5
Ability to critique peer counselor's work	1	2	3	4	5
Ability to express suggestions and opinions with respect	1	2	3	4	5
Ability to receive feedback from peers	1	2	3	4	5
Ability to generalize indirect feelings from the supervision of peer counselors	1	2	3	4	5
Other ________________________	1	2	3	4	5

Reprinted from Borders, L. D., & Leddick, G. R. (1987). *Handbook of counseling supervision* (p. 11). Alexandria, VA: Association for Counselor Education and Supervision.

individual variations underlie both the challenge and the joy of conducting supervision.

Supervision Frameworks

We begin with supervision models because they provide frameworks for organizing knowledge and skills for conducting supervision. Much like counseling theories, supervision models serve as a guide for choosing an intervention for a particular supervisee and session and for evaluating one's effectiveness as a supervisor. Two models offer different and highly complementary perspectives on the supervision enterprise.

Discrimination Model

Bernard's (1979, 1997) discrimination model not only is one of the best known models of supervision, it also has strong empirical support (Ellis & Dell, 1986). In addition, it is a model that can be viewed—and taught—at simple and complex levels, depending on the readiness of the supervisor. What appears at first glance to be a simple grid actually has multiple applications, nuances, and subtleties. The discrimination model forms a matrix or grid of supervisor roles—teacher, counselor, and consultant—and supervision foci (see Table 1.4). Bernard has used several terms for the three foci; our labels are different from hers, but we believe they are in the true spirit of her ideas.

Table 1.4 Discrimination Model Matrix (With Examples)

Supervision Focus Areas	*Supervisor Roles*		
	Teacher	*Counselor*	*Consultant*
Counseling Performance Skills	Help counselor practice confrontation skills, paradoxical intervention, positive reframing, or gestalt two-chair technique.	Work on skills needed to respond to a client's challenges, delivered in an empathic manner.	Help counselor generate ideas about other interventions that might work with a client.
Cognitive Counseling Skills	How does a family history of substance abuse influence the client's current behavior?	Reframe client's challenging behaviors as self-protection.	Work on understanding why a particular intervention didn't work with a family.
Self-awareness	Explain how counselor's reactions to client are informative about the client's self-presentation.	Help counselor identify feelings of defensiveness in response to a client's challenging behaviors.	Respond to counselor's request to explore negative feelings about a client.
Professional Behaviors	Explain how an ethical standard applies to a client situation.	Explore counselor's conflicting feelings about needing to break confidentiality.	In an ethical situation, help generate options for responding to a client.

Based on Bernard (1979), Borders and Benshoff (1999), and Lanning (1986).

In addition, we have included a fourth focus area identified by Lanning (1986; Lanning & Freeman, 1994).

What we refer to as *counseling performance skills* denotes what a counselor *does* during a counseling session, including basic and advanced helping skills (e.g., empathic responding, confrontation, immediacy), theoretically based techniques (e.g., circular questioning, reframing, dream analysis, two-chair exercise), procedural skills (e.g., opening and closing a session), and issue-specific skills (e.g., suicide assessment). *Cognitive counseling skills* refer to how a counselor *thinks* before, during, and after a session. Within this category, supervisors most commonly focus on case conceptualization, the construction of a comprehensive explanation of a client and the client's issues that holds together. A strong case conceptualization is built on recognition of themes and patterns. This focus area also includes a counselor's moment-to-moment thought processes during a session—observing and assessing what is happening, what is needed, options for responding and intervening, and evaluating one's efforts. *Self-awareness* involves a supervisee's recognition of personal issues, beliefs, and motivations that may influence in-session behavior as well as case conceptualization. A supervisee's personal background can affect his or her perceptions and create an overly positive or overly negative view of a client, create distance from or identification with a client, lead to overly prescriptive interventions or a sense of being stuck about how to help a client, and otherwise cloud a supervisee's objectivity regarding a client. *Professional behaviors* refer to adherence to ethical, legal, and professional guidelines as well as appropriate on-site behaviors (e.g., punctuality, following protocols for case notes and emergency client situations).

According to Bernard (1979, 1997), supervisors may address each of the four focus areas from each of the three roles of teacher, counselor, and consultant. Importantly, the supervisor does not literally move into a pure teacher, counselor, or consultant role. Instead, the supervisor draws on the knowledge and skills endemic to each role. For example, drawing on the teacher role, a supervisor's primary goal is to instruct. This does not necessarily mean, however, that the supervisor lectures or tells, a portrayal of this role that we often have heard and seen. A good classroom teacher doesn't just lecture, but understands the importance of using a variety of instructional interventions that tap into a student's various learning modalities (e.g., reading, hearing, doing). In fact, experiential learning activities are quite appropriate for teaching counseling skills, and also are critical to solidifying learning. A supervisor certainly may need to explain a concept, or tell a supervisee the steps of a counseling technique, or even correct a supervisee's understanding of a theory or diagnosis. The supervisor also will recognize the teaching–learning process in many other interventions (these are discussed in chaps. 3 and 4, this volume).

In drawing from the teacher role, the supervisor also is drawing on well-established principles of learning theory. For example, we know that students can take in only so much information during one teaching block. For a 1-hour session, supervisors typically can expect to cover no more than three points—perhaps fewer, depending on the complexity of the concepts involved.

The counselor role also provides the supervisor with critical skills for educating supervisees. Obviously, the content of this role is what you are trying to impart to the supervisee, but this is only the first level of applying one's counseling skills in supervision. Importantly, the supervisor does not become the supervisee's counselor; such a role violates ethical standards (see chap. 6 and Appendix C, this volume; see also Whiston & Emerson, 1989) due to conflicting expectations (e.g., nonjudgmental treatment vs. instruction and evaluation). Rather, a supervisor uses counseling skills to understand, motivate, and relate to the supervisee. One's counseling background is particularly helpful in assessing a supervisee's "problems about learning" (Ekstein & Wallerstein, 1972). Given the dynamics of human nature, we can expect that all supervisees truly want to learn about being a better counselor *and* that they all truly fear what they will learn about themselves along the way. A supervisor's counseling background provides an understanding that this dynamic is normal and that it must be addressed if the supervisee is to begin to develop his or her potential as a counselor, as well as interventions for helping the supervisee recognize and surmount fears regarding the change inherent in one's growth and development.

We want to make clear that it is certainly okay to address supervisees' personal issues; after all, self-awareness is one of the focus areas in the discrimination model and thus key to total development of a counselor. The focus, however, is on how to contain personal issues so that they do not interfere with a supervisees' work with a client rather than resolve those issues. This distinction, however, is not always clear in practice; in fact, it often seems more of a wavering gray space than a clean demarcation line. Given the ambiguity of this distinction, as well as ethical implications for overstepping into a counselor role, it is not surprising that many new supervisors tend to be somewhat reluctant, if not skittish, about addressing supervisees' personal issues (Borders & Fong, 1994). Helping new supervisors develop decision points regarding the appropriateness of addressing personal issues in a particular situation, as well as their comfort in doing so, is a critical task for the trainer or supervisor of supervisors.

Drawing from the counselor role, the supervisor's awareness of content and process are particularly critical to working with a supervisee. Clearly, helping a supervisee recognize both content and process in counseling sessions is a supervision goal. More to the point here, the supervisor is just as attuned to process dynamics within the supervision session, such as a supervisee's self-presentation (Friedlander, Keller, Peca-Baker, & Olk, 1986) and response to questions, when a supervisee is fully engaged versus self-protective, body language and other nonverbal messages (e.g., laughter). Drawing attention to process within the supervision relationship is one powerful way of addressing the supervisee's "problems about learning." Indeed, the supervisory relationship itself often becomes the learning tool, and a supervisor's counseling-based knowledge and skills are a major resource for this work.

Empirically, the consultant role is the least distinct role (Ellis & Dell, 1986); it appears to be an underlying dynamic of the other roles and much of a supervisor's behavior. Most supervisors prefer a collaborative (over an authoritarian) relationship with their supervisees, and this collaborative nature is a marker of the consultant's approach. A supervisor drawing from the consultant role, then, helps the supervisee brainstorm possible explanations for a client's behavior and appropriate interventions, as well as any new skills the counselor needs to be effective with the client. This supervisor also is observing the supervisee's ability and willingness to engage in a collaborative relationship.

Some roles seem best suited for a particular focus area. The teacher role, for example, seems the logical match for addressing counseling performance skills, and the counselor role seems a perfect match for enhancing a supervisee's self-awareness. Bernard (Bernard & Goodyear, 1998) purported, however, that any role can be applied to any focus area, and we agree. The key in choosing a role is consideration of the goals of the supervisor. For example, is the goal to have the supervisee practice a new skill (teacher role) or recognize and experience reactions to a client (counselor role)? Does the situation call for the supervisee to use a particular skill (e.g., suicide assessment, teacher role) or is there room for the supervisee to identify several appropriate interventions (consultant role)?

We also have found that the role–foci combinations can be used for a variety of purposes throughout the course of a supervision experience. Most commonly, a supervisor chooses a role and focus area as the basis for an intervention designed to create change, such as practicing a new skill (teacher role/performance skills), expanding case conceptualization of a client to include family dynamics (teacher or consultant role/cognitive counseling skills), and exploring a supervisee's reluctance to confront a particular client when this skill has been evidenced with other clients (counselor or consultant role/self-awareness). The discrimination model, however, is just as appropriate and effective toward goals of assessment and evaluation of a supervisee. A supervisor may gain assessment data through observation of a supervisee's response to a question or request. Does the supervisee identify thoughts in response to a "how do you feel" question (counselor role/self-awareness)? What case conceptualization components are included in the supervisee's explanation of a client's issue (consultant role/cognitive counseling skills)? How well does the supervisee perform a particular skill in a role-play with the supervisor (teacher role/performance skills)?

An important lesson highlighted by the discrimination model, then, is that a supervisor must be flexible and intentional. The supervisor needs to be ready to employ any of the three roles toward any of the four focus areas, at any point during the supervision session, toward a particular goal or goals (e.g., assessment, change intervention, evaluation). A supervisor is compelled, then, to self-assess knowledge and skills as well as comfort level within each role and focus area. All of us have preferences, based on our experiences and felt competence in a role or focus area. For example, we have found that experienced counselors in our training groups often discount the teacher role and tend to think of their supervisees in clinical terms. As a result, they often slip too far into counselor–client interactions with their supervisees. Supervisors with a teaching background typically are more comfortable with their evaluative responsibilities and often overlook process in the pursuit of content (see also Borders, 1992).

Our preferences also are influenced by our beliefs concerning which are most critical for learning and change. These beliefs are rooted in our theoretical orientation and broader philosophical outlook (Friedlander & Ward, 1984). As Bernard and Goodyear (1998) noted, "Supervisors never can or will divorce themselves totally from the influence of their theoretical beliefs" (p. 30). Some supervisors, then, will assert that self-awareness is the key to supervisee growth and development, whereas others will give first attention to changing a supervisee's behaviors or skills, believing that changes in feelings and cognitions necessarily will follow. All are correct—depending on the supervisee, the client, the clinical issue, and the supervisory relationship.

It is paramount, then, for supervisors to acknowledge their beliefs and preferences and consider how they translate into both strengths and limitations in their work with supervisees. If you are in a supervisor training group, it is likely that a variety of beliefs and preferences are represented by group members. If so, take advantage of the opportunity to learn from each other in practice activities and review of supervision sessions.

In practice, the roles and focus areas are not as distinct as they are in theory. A particular statement by a supervisor may reflect more than one role and tap into more than one focus area. Human behavior is rarely as simple as any one theoretical explanation or model. Nevertheless, we believe the discrimination model provides an invaluable framework for understanding the work of a supervisor, and is an instructive point of departure for anyone seeking to become a supervisor for the first time—or those seeking to enhance their existing knowledge, skills, and self-awareness as a supervisor. Finally, we applaud the implied demand that a supervisor be both flexible and intentional. Clearly, supervision requires much thought, preparation, and planning, as well as execution of sculpted interventions and the evaluation of them. The intentional and deliberate educational process characterizing effective supervision will be recurring themes throughout this *New Handbook*.

Developmental Models

Developmental models burst upon the scene in the early 1980s, stimulating a renewed interest in supervision and an explosion of empirical studies. These models provided a transcending view of counselor growth within supervision, as opposed to more theory-specific approaches (e.g., Dewald, 1987; Patterson, 1983; Schmidt, 1979; Wessler & Ellis, 1980) that, many agreed, treated supervision as an adjunct to therapy rather than a unique, educational enterprise. Developmental models had immediate intuitive appeal, as they seemed to reflect many supervisors' experiences over the years, and the models' positive, growth-oriented perspectives were attractive to practitioners, given the developmental orientation of the field. As the term *development* suggests, the models are sequential and hierarchial, progressing toward greater complexity and integration.

Unlike the discrimination model, there is no one, uniform schema for developmental models. Of the most well-known theoretical models, they vary in number of and labels for stages, as well as emphasis, with some focusing on cognitive development (e.g., Blocher, 1983; Stoltenberg, 1981) and others offering a broader psychosocial perspective (e.g., Loganbill, Hardy, & Delworth, 1982). An empirically based model (Rønnestad & Skovholt, 1993; Skovholt & Rønnestad, 1992a, 1992b) provides a broader perspective of counselor development along eight categories that include conceptual and affective domains as well as working style, preferred learning processes, and sources of influence. Nevertheless, there is much similarity in the themes, behaviors, motivations, and developmental progression described in the models, as well as the supervisory environments suggested for various points along the development continuum. Thus, we provide a summary description of developmental models rather than descriptions of each individual model.

Importantly, developmental models indicate that counselor growth continues across the lifespan. In fact, higher levels of development are achieved in no less than 20 to 30 years. In addition, a critical point in the models is that supervisees' general level of development (e.g., conceptual functioning: Harvey, Hunt, & Schroder, 1961; ego functioning: Loevinger, 1976) govern their rate of progress through the stages and limit their capacity to achieve the higher levels of functioning. Supervisees can not view clients with greater complexity than they view other persons in their world, and counselors' developmental stages are not equivalent to their experience levels (Borders, 2001). In fact, one model (Loganbill et al., 1982) suggests counselors recycle through stages and issues at greater levels of complexity. Graduate training lays an important foundation, then, but some of a counselor's most significant growth occurs after graduation, providing the counselor is open to further growth and has the appropriate and necessary supervisory environment. In addition, although there is general support for the tenets of developmental models (Borders, 1989; Stoltenberg, McNeill, & Crethar, 1994; Worthington, 1987), most research to date has been focused primarily on earlier stages of development. We have few details regarding postdegree supervision and counselor development.

Supervisees at early stages of development are characterized by black-and-white thinking and broad, somewhat simplistic, categorical understandings of their clients. Both their thinking and behavior can be fairly rigid. Great attention is given to "rules" and the one "right" way to think and behave. For example, all divorced women are assumed to have quite similar issues and needs, and therefore receive the same interventions. Relatedly, beginning supervisees have little awareness of their strengths, weaknesses, and motivations, and lack confidence in their skills. They are often highly anxious in supervision.

Supervisees in middle stages of confusion (Loganbill et al., 1982) or conditional dependence/autonomy (Skovholt & Rønnestad, 1992b; Stoltenberg, 1981) have more differentiated perceptions of clients, as they have begun recognizing individual differences among clients with the same presenting issue. Thus, they are more flexible and variable, and more individualized, in their interventions and treatment plans. These supervisees have greater confidence and fairly consistent awareness of their strengths and limitations, although they experience a bit of a roller-coaster sense of themselves as counselors when they face a new clinical issue or client characteristic. Interestingly, the developmental models imply that most counselors likely are in these middle stages when they graduate and obtain their first professional positions.

In the later stages of integration (Loganbill et al., 1982) and integrity (Skovholt & Rønnestad, 1992b), supervisees' client conceptualizations are both more comprehensive and more specific to a particular client. They are comfortable with the polarities and paradoxes inherent in clinical work, and consider more sophisticated dynamics in human relationships (e.g., the mutual and circular influences within a family). Their interventions often are creative, and are based in clinical "wisdom" (Skovholt & Rønnestad, 1992b) based in both theory and their own accumulated experience-based knowledge. Integration of professional and personal identities has been achieved.

The strong cognitive basis for the developmental models is perhaps clearest in Blocher's (1983) description of the "very high level of cognitive functioning" characteristic of those at the highest levels of development:

> This functioning includes the ability to take multiple perspectives in order to achieve empathic understanding with people who hold a variety of world views, value systems and personal constructs. It includes the ability to differentiate among and manipulate a wide range and large number of relevant facts and causal factors. Finally, it involves the ability to integrate and synthesize in creative or unusual ways large amounts of such information to arrive at an understanding of the psychological identity and life situation of a wide range of other human beings. Still further the counselor engages in this quest in active collaboration with the client, and in the hope of imparting some skill and understanding of the process to the client. (Blocher, 1983, p. 28)

The cognitive shifts across stages are accompanied by analogous changes in the supervisory relationship. Supervisees move from dependency to autonomy, with middle stages of conditional reliance on the supervisor, characterized by conflict and tension. They move from great anxiety to firm and realistic confidence.

The cognitive, affective, and relationship dynamics at different developmental stages provide guidance regarding the supervisory methods appropriate to each stage. The optimal environment (Stoltenberg, 1981) is a mismatch of about one-half step beyond the supervisee's current functioning, so that the supervisee receives adequate challenge balanced by adequate support. Supervisors of beginning supervisees, then, are primarily instructional and skill focused. They provide the structure and direction, the modeling and explaining, needed by the novice supervisee, along with large doses of support and encouragement.

At the middle stages, supervisors are more focused on the person of the supervisee and more prone to use the supervisory relationship as a learning vehicle. Middle-stage supervisees are more open to—and even welcome or request—discussions about their reactions to clients, including transference and countertransference issues and parallel process dynamics. They invite attention to their personal issues that impact their professional work. Supervisors, then, are more confrontive and immediate, as well as more respectful of the supervisee's growing independence. They highlight the process in counseling and supervision sessions. They help their supervisees generalize their learnings, question their assumptions and hypotheses, and seek multiple sources of feedback about their work. At the same time, supervisors are ready to be supportive and even instructional when a supervisee faces a new or overwhelming situation.

In the latter developmental stages, supervisors approach their supervisees in a more collegial fashion, helping supervisees think through their choices and options and see themes and patterns across clients and sessions. They assume the supervisee will identify areas to be addressed during supervision, respecting the supervisee's movement from external to internal evaluative criteria and feedback. They are mentors regarding the supervisee's creation of an integrated personal and professional identity.

Within each of these general descriptions of optimal developmental environments, a supervisor makes adjustments as needed, based on the individual needs and characteristics of the supervisee, as well as the clinical issues and culture of the counseling environment. These additional issues are discussed in more detail in chapter 3 (this volume).

The descriptions of optimal supervisory environments may sound familiar, as most of the prescribed supervisor behaviors can be placed within the matrix of the discrimination model. Indeed, developmental models provide the rationale for choosing a supervisor role and focus area for a particular supervisee at a specific point in time. Developmental models suggest a teacher, counselor, consultant sequence across a supervisee's development, with more emphasis on counseling performance skills in early stages and more attention to cognitive counseling skills and self-awareness (at greater and greater depth) in middle and later stages. Together, these two supervision models provide a comprehensive and instructive framework for conducting effective supervision for counselors at any point in their development.

Within the developmental models, supervisors clearly have a proactive role. To be effective, supervisors actively assess their supervisees to determine which stage and developmental issues are present. A supervision plan, with the appropriate mismatch of challenge and support, is devised based on that assessment. Loganbill et al. (1982) further suggested that the supervisor identify what issues need to be introduced by the supervisor. Using their model (Table 1.5), supervisors first determine the stage of awareness (stagnation, confusion, integration) a supervisee has achieved along eight critical issues

Table 1.5 Assessment of Supervisee Developmental Level

Critical Issues in Supervision	*Stage 1 Stagnation Stability*	*Stage 2 Confusion*	*Stage 3 Integration*
1. *Issues of Competence.* Skills. Technique. Mastery. Ability to take appropriate action.			
2. *Issues of Emotional Awareness.* Knowing oneself. Differentiation of feelings. Ability to use own reactions/emotions diagnostically.			
3. *Issues of Autonomy.* Sense of one's own choices/decisions. Independence and self-directedness to appropriate degree. Sense of self.			
4. *Issues of Identity.* Theoretical consistency. Conceptual integration. Sense of self as therapist/counselor.			
5. *Issues of Respect for Individual Differences.* Deep and basic respect. Active effort to understand. Appreciation of differences.			
6. *Issues of Purpose and Direction.* Formulation of treatment plan and appropriate long- and short-term goals. Cognitive map of client progress.			
7. *Issues of Personal Motivation.* Personal drives and meaning. Reward satisfaction. Complex and evolving nature of motivation.			
8. *Issues of Professional Ethics.* Legal issues. Values. Professional standards. Integration of these into ongoing practice.			

Reprinted from Borders, L. D., & Leddick, G. R. (1987). *Handbook of counseling supervision* (p. 22). Alexandria, VA: Association for Counselor Education and Supervision.

(e.g., competence, autonomy, purpose and direction, emotional awareness). Priority is given to issues found to be at the confusion stage because these likely are occupying the supervisee's energy and attention. Should there be few critical issues at this stage, the supervisor begins to consider which issues might be pushed into confusion (i.e., which the supervisee seems ready to and capable of addressing, which are particularly salient for the supervisee's clients and setting, etc.). In this way, the supervisor proactively encourages counselor growth while managing the number of developmental issues at play during a particular supervisory experience. The further implication is that the supervisor must be ready to provide appropriate interventions across the developmental span. Again, as demanded by the discrimination model, a supervisor is flexible, intentional, and proactive.

Summary

One goal of this chapter is to help you learn to think like a supervisor (Borders, 1992; Borders & Benshoff, 1999). We have tried to illustrate how you translate your previous professional training into behaviors appropriate to your supervisory role. Further explanations and practice exercises are provided in two multimedia products. "Learning to Think Like a Supervisor" (Borders & Benshoff, 1999) is a training video produced by the Association for Counselor Education and Supervision (available from the American Counseling Association). It includes vignettes illustrating the roles and focus areas in the discrimination model (Bernard, 1979, 1997) as well as discussion of developmental models. A more extensive training package is found in "Clinical Supervisor Training: An Interactive CD-ROM Training Program for the Helping Professions" (Baltimore & Crutchfield, 2003). A solid grounding in the discrimination model and the counselor developmental perspectives is needed for the following chapters, and these two training products can be helpful in solidifying your learning.

Discussion Questions

1. Complete one or more of the various self-assessments suggested in this chapter. Discuss your results with a colleague or your supervision instructor. Then, based on the results, write three to five learning goals for your next supervision experience.
2. Which supervisor role do you think you likely will use the most in your next supervision experience? Which focus area do you think is your preference?
3. Which role(s) and focus area(s) were used most often in your experiences as a supervisee? Why do you think those particular ones were used? Did they change over time?

4. Can you remember some of your early conceptualizations of clients? How did they reflect the categorical, black-white thinking characteristic of beginning counselors? What supervision (and other) experiences helped you move toward more sophisticated understandings of your clients?
5. What examples of developmental thinking and interacting have you observed in your own supervisees?

Chapter 2

Initial Supervisory Sessions

First impressions are important, and this is certainly true of first supervision sessions as well. Similar to first counseling sessions and first classroom meetings, supervisors need to approach initial sessions with a supervisee with some deliberate attention to the purpose and goals to be addressed. There are both important procedural tasks and contextual and relationship issues that need to be addressed. In the initial session, a supervisor sets the tone for the rest of the supervisory experience. Thus, it is prudent for you to plan carefully—intentionally—for this first meeting. Think ahead to the close of this initial session: What do you want your supervisee to be thinking and feeling when he or she leaves? After the first session, how do you want the supervisee to describe his or her anticipations about working with you to a colleague and fellow student? For some supervisors, *friendly and supportive* may be high on their list. For others, *challenging but fair* may be the preferred descriptor. It may be that you would have different goals based on the supervisee (e.g., developmental or experience level, previous interactions with the supervisee in another context).

We caution you not to make too many assumptions about your supervisee based on other supervisors' reports or even your previous experience with the supervisee. The supervisory setting is unique, quite different from the classroom setting, for example, and it may be that your supervisee is more or less comfortable in a one-to-one supervisory relationship (or group supervision) than a large class. Similarly, a fresh start with you may make this supervision experience quite different from reports of previous experiences. So, although you certainly should use previous experiences to inform your plans for the initial session, also make sure you haven't predecided how it will go. Remain objective and open to new perspectives and interactions with the supervisee. At the least, you have a fresh opportunity to create a new relationship with your supervisee.

Whenever possible, schedule the initial supervisory session before your supervisee begins seeing clients. This allows you to focus on setting parameters, clarifying expectations, and establishing a working relationship without

DOI: 10.4324/9781003251583-2

the pressures or distractions of client needs and clinical questions. In settings away from a university, this may not be possible.

Procedural Tasks

There are some tasks and topics that should be on your agenda for any initial supervision session. First, by the end of this session there should be a clear contract between you and your supervisee regarding how this experience will be conducted. A written contract, signed by both the supervisor and supervisee, is recommended by some professionals (McCarthy et al., 1995; Osborn & Davis, 1996; Remley & Herlihy, 2001). In a university setting, this contract might be in the form of a syllabus. For site supervisors of interns or supervisors of post-degree counselors, a contract may need to be created. Our recent experience is that some internship sites (especially medical settings) have become quite specific about the content of a contract; these new contracts are influenced by recent federal legislation, particularly the Health Insurance Portability and Accountability Act (HIPAA).

At a minimum, the supervisory contract should address the following:

1. The number and frequency of meetings, and when these will occur, as well as how you will contact each other if a session needs to be rescheduled.
2. How each of you is expected to prepare for supervision sessions. What information (in what format) should the supervisee provide for you (and when is this due)?
3. Is the selection of sessions for review up to the supervisee, or do you have some parameters for choosing (e.g., one initial counseling session, one closure session, one group session, two consecutive sessions for at least one client, etc.)?
4. What kinds of experiences (if any) the supervisee should complete, as appropriate to the setting (e.g., lead a minimum of one group, conduct at least one classroom guidance unit, participate in in-home family sessions).
5. What professional behaviors are expected (e.g., case notes are to be completed within what timeframe after a session, which staff meetings the supervisee should attend, being on time, etc.).
6. What supervisory interventions you will or may use.
7. In particular, the use of audio or videotapes needs to be addressed, including an appropriate client consent form that states how the tapes will be used in supervision and, ultimately, disposed of or erased, and how client confidentiality will be maintained. Some decisions regarding whether counseling tapes or case notes can be mailed or e-mailed to you also needs to be addressed (see chap. 6, this volume, for further discussion of these issues). Be sure to state that you need audible tapes, and indicate whether you will accept microsized tapes.

8. How the supervisee will be evaluated. Both formative and summative evaluations need to be addressed. What type of ongoing feedback will you provide? We have colleagues who provide written commentaries for each tape. These commentaries help them plan for the session and allow the supervisee to review the feedback whenever they wish. Others take notes for themselves and plan from these but do not provide any written summaries to the supervisee. Whether verbal or written, the feedback format should be an appropriate match for your supervisee's needs. It's also important to provide the supervisee with a copy of any assessment tool you will use, such as a midterm or final evaluation form, or the format required by the licensure board, the employer or agency, and so forth. Supervisees have a right to know how they will be evaluated (see chaps. 6 and 7 for further discussion), and knowing the criteria upfront can help lessen their anxiety about the evaluative aspect of the supervision process also.
9. What the supervisee should do in case of an emergency. Agencies typically have written policies, which should be shared with the supervisee. If you are a university supervisor of an intern, this may involve notifying site supervisors first and following the site's emergency procedures. Be clear when and how you are to be notified, and what your role and responsibilities are in these situations.
10. Fee per session, if applicable, and how and when this is to be paid.

Much of this more procedural information can be covered in a professional disclosure statement. McCarthy et al. (1995) provided an example of such an agreement. The example statements we have provided in Tables 2.1 and 2.2 were written for supervision conducted in private practice, but they can be adapted for other settings.

You may not know your stance on all of these procedural points yet. Most are covered in some detail in subsequent chapters. We chose to include these questions here to alert you to the kind of decisions you need to make, and thus inform your reading of the rest of the *New Handbook*.

Learning Goals

A second type of contract involves the supervisee's learning goals. We suggest this be a separate document from the "must do" more procedural tasks previously outlined. Learning goals are supervisees' best guess of what they need and want to focus on during supervision. These goals are negotiable, and may change based on the issues raised by clients or other issues that surface during the supervision experience. It has been our experience that a supervisee's learning goals are on target for what we need to work on, and that additional goals will surface.

Supervisees vary in their ability to state realistic, concrete, and specific goals. Beginning supervisees, in particular, have a limited basis of information

Table 2.1 Professional Disclosure Statement for Supervision

SUPERVISEE DISCLOSURE STATEMENT (INFORMATION AND CONSENT)

I am pleased that you have selected me as your clinical supervisor. This document is designed to inform you about my background and to ensure that you understand our professional relationship.

I hold a PhD in Counselor Education and Supervision from the University of North Carolina at Greensboro, degree being received in 1995. I was a professional school counselor 1988–1992, and have been a Licensed Professional Counselor since 1995 (in North Carolina, and now in Georgia). I am also a National Certified Counselor, and a National Certified School Counselor. I am in the process of applying for the Approved Clinical Supervisor credential, administered through the National Board for Certified Counselors.

SUPERVISION SERVICES OFFERED/MODELS USED

Professional counselors can always benefit from continued professional development, and clinical supervision is one important way to promote self-assessment and development. Below I will describe my approach to counseling (as this may affect my interventions as your supervisor) as well as my preferred model of clinical supervision.

In working with children as an elementary school counselor, I believed strongly in encouragement of the client's strengths, and in making a plan for action, then accepting no excuses when the client chose not to follow up. My belief in Adlerian goals of misbehavior and my use of Reality Therapy contracts with clients served me well as a school counselor. In my experience with adults, I have found that I prefer a more person-centered approach, though I will still use goals and contracts when appropriate. I believe that people are searching for a purpose in life, and that there are numerous, valid ways that counselors can help them strive for that purpose.

Supervision includes your active involvement as well as efforts to improve your counseling skills and abilities. You will have to work both in and out of the supervision sessions. You will be asked to make tapes (audio or video) of your counseling sessions, so that we (I and the group of your peers) might examine your skills and give you constructive feedback. Sometimes change will be easy and swift, but more often it will be slow and deliberate; effort may need to be repeated.

I take a developmental approach to clinical supervision. Counselors who are not continuously growing and developing both personally and professionally can become stagnant, and often do more harm than good with their clients. And, while much can be gained by attending workshops and conferences, the real work begins when counselors turn inward, examining their own skills, as well as sharpening themselves as tools within the counseling session. As a clinical supervisor, I see my role as one to provide challenge and support while you look inside yourself in just this way.

If we are to work together we will need to specify goals, methods, risks and benefits of supervision, the approximate time commitment involved, costs and other aspects of your particular situation. Before going further, I expect us to agree on a plan to which we will both adhere. Periodically, we will evaluate our progress and redesign our goals if needed.

(Continued)

Table 2.1 (Continued)

As with any powerful intervention, there are both benefits and risks associated with participating in clinical supervision. Risks might include feeling strong anxiety upon being "evaluated," or experiencing uncomfortable levels of feelings such as anger, guilt, or sadness when working through your own issues which might affect your abilities to successfully function as a professional counselor. If you are willing to take these risks, I believe that the benefits of personal and professional growth will far outweigh the fleeting discomfort.

The particular approach to peer group clinical supervision which I use is called the Borders Model. Within this model, presenting supervisees share segments of taped counseling sessions, asking specific questions for feedback. Their peers review the tape from within specified roles (e.g., client, counselor, teacher, parent ...) and give their feedback using first-person "I language." You will see a training tape on this model of supervision during our initial group supervision session.

CONFIDENTIALITY

I regard the information you share with me with great respect, so I want us to be as clear as possible about how it will be handled. Because our supervision will be conducted within a group, I cannot guarantee the complete privacy of our conversations. I will not share anything outside of our group, unless I am ethically and/or legally required to do so.

EXPLANATION OF DUAL RELATIONSHIPS

As fellow professionals, we may encounter each other in numerous ways outside of these supervision sessions. Please help me maintain an appropriately professional relationship as supervisor and supervisee within our sessions. These professional boundaries are needed in order for you to receive the most benefit from our time together.

COMPLAINT PROCEDURES

If you are dissatisfied with any aspect of our work, please inform me immediately. This will make our work together more efficient and effective. If you have any questions, feel free to ask. Please sign and date both copies of this form, as well as the attached Letter of Agreement. A copy for your records will be returned to you. I will retain a copy in my confidential records.

Supervisor's signature　　　　　　Date

Supervisee's signature　　　　　　Date

---

to draw from. They likely have had little feedback about their counseling work. Their knowledge of all the skills, techniques, and theories they might use is still being developed, and they may not yet be aware of some of their own issues that may affect their work with clients. Even advanced supervisees may have some difficulty expressing specific and concrete goals. A listing of counseling behaviors, appropriate to the supervisee's developmental level and counseling setting, can provide a starting point for identifying learning goals. If you are using an evaluation form that includes such a list, it can be a useful

Table 2.2 Letter of Agreement for Private Practice Supervision

LETTER OF AGREEMENT

Lori L. Brown (to be known hereafter as "the supervisor") agrees to provide the undersigned person (to be known hereafter as "the supervisee") with certain services in exchange for certain payment, as outlined below.

The supervisor will provide one three-hour session of clinical group supervision per month over a period of ten months, for a total of 30 hours of face-to-face clinical supervision time. This will be sufficient for the supervisee to claim one year of directed experience in his/her attempt to achieve the status of Licensed Professional Counselor in the state of Georgia. This agreement will begin on the date written below, and end no later than June 15, 2005.

In exchange for this service, the supervisee will pay the amount of **$25.00 per hour,** for a total of **$75.00 per three-hour session** of clinical supervision. The supervisor will bill the supervisee for this payment on a monthly basis, with payment due prior to the monthly supervision session. The first bill will cover both the first and the second supervision sessions. Each bill will be mailed to the supervisee on or near the first day of the month.

The supervisor is not responsible for rescheduling group sessions when the supervisee must miss a session. In the event that the supervisee must miss a group session, the supervisor agrees to provide, in replacement for the three hours of clinical group supervision, three hours of individual clinical supervision, at the cost of $70.00 per hour. The supervisee understands that he/she will not be able to claim one year of directed experience if he/she does not complete a total of 30 hours of face-to-face clinical supervision time, and agrees to the above arrangement as a contingency plan, in case of a missed group supervision session.

____

Supervisor's signature Date

____

Supervisee's signature Date

exercise to have the supervisee complete an initial self-rating on that form as the basis for identifying and even prioritizing learning goals (and a comparative self-evaluation at the end of the supervision experience; see also chap. 7, this volume).

We also have found that the discrimination model can be very effective in helping beginning and advanced supervisees identify relevant goals. The four focus areas in the model (i.e., counseling process skills, cognitive counseling skills, self-awareness, and professional behaviors; see Table 1.1) suggest to the supervisee the broad spectrum of areas involved in becoming an effective counselor, and make clear that all four areas are appropriate topics for supervision sessions. A supervisee, then, might be asked to write one to three goal statements for each of the four focus areas in the discrimination model.

Even with these aids, supervisees typically will need some help in stating their goals in concrete, specific, and even operational terms. Some questioning

("What would you be doing differently?" or "How would that look in a session?" or "What would you be feeling before a session?" or "What would you be saying to yourself instead?") and discussion may be necessary to help a supervisee clarify and better focus learning goals—and to be sure that both of you understand what the goal means. *Being more confrontive*, for example, is a frequent goal that means at least several different things to supervisees. Relatedly, *leading three psychoeducational groups* is not a goal, but part of the contract for work or experiences expected or required at the site. *Using more experiential activities* or *Becoming more aware of and commenting on group process* would be learning goals related to leading the psychoeducational groups. Part of your responsibility here is to make sure supervisees' goals are realistic, appropriate to their developmental level, and attainable in the particular counseling setting.

If supervisees often have some difficulty writing specific, concrete goals, why spend the time and effort on this task? First, the exercise of identifying and writing learning goals helps supervisees take some ownership for the learning process. In setting goals for themselves, they are required to reflect on their counseling work—feedback they received, their comfort level with various clients, the areas they often forget in conceptualizing a client. In establishing learning goals, they also have the opportunity to state what areas of growth they already have achieved and what strengths they bring to the current supervision experience. Your attention to a supervisee's self-stated goals also is a tangible sign of your interest in knowing what the supervisee wants from working with you, and your desire for a collaborative working relationship.

In stating their goals, a supervisee also has given you permission to address those goals, and provided you with an entree and the words to use. A supervisee can state a goal and then be reluctant to bring it up and actually address it during supervision. Now you, the supervisor, can bring it up: "In listening to your tape, I remembered your goal about being more confrontive. I think I have found a section of the session where we can work on that today." Although this approach doesn't totally eliminate a supervisee's anxiety about working on a particular goal, we have found that it is easier for supervisees to hear the feedback when it is phrased within their own goals and words. This is also another way of expressing your respect and interest in the supervisee's goals. Similarly, the supervisee's learning goals become the basis for periodic *checkups*—formative feedback regarding progress made toward each goal, which goals have not yet been addressed. Such a review may indicate that some goals need to be restated, dropped, or even checked off, and others need to be added. In addition, supervisees know where they stand when goals are reviewed periodically, and so there are no surprises at the end—for the supervisee or the supervisor. Learning goals, then, also become one basis for the final, summative evaluation.

We note that the emphasis on a supervisee's self-stated goals does not restrict us as supervisors from setting other goals for the supervisee. Supervisor-initiated goals may come out of the supervisee's work with clients—a skill or issue that the supervisee did not recognize or anticipate—or from the supervisory relationship (i.e., lessen the supervisee's anxiety or dependence on the supervisor, curb the supervisee's verbage and overreporting of details). Depending on the goal, the supervisor may or may not share the goal with the supervisee. A supervisor might not announce that decreasing the supervisee's anxiety about receiving feedback is a goal but might remark at some point that the supervisee seems less anxious (and, in essence, congratulating the supervisee for achieving this goal).

Relationship Tasks

Clearly, attention to procedural tasks, such as a working contract and learning goals, provide one vehicle for establishing the tone of a supervisory relationship. Specific attention to some contextual and relationship issues also is needed during the initial supervisory session. A strong and positive working relationship will enhance the supervision experience and serve as a buffer for those challenging moments that inevitably will occur.

Discussion of learning goals quite naturally can lead to discussion of the supervisee's learning style and preferences for supervision. Supervisees might be asked to share what has and has not worked for them (from their perspective) in previous supervisory relationships and their hopes for this supervision experience. Supervisors, of course, must respond to any unrealistic or inappropriate requests. Similarly, supervisors can share relevant experiences as a counselor (e.g., in a similar setting with similar clients) and supervisor (e.g., what you particularly enjoy about the supervision process). If possible, some statement about what you are looking forward to in this particular supervision experience also is helpful, including your anticipation that you will be learning from the supervisee as well.

The initial session is also the appropriate time to put diversity issues on the table, and it is critical that the supervisor take the first step (Brown & Landrum-Brown, 1995; Constantine, 1997; Fong, 1994). In fact, supervisor-initiated, early discussions of multicultural issues, in a safe and open manner, have a positive impact on the supervisory relationship and working alliance, and supervisee satisfaction with supervision, particularly in crosscultural supervision dyads (Duan & Roehlke, 2001; Gatmon et al., 2001).

Hird, Cavalieri, Dulko, Felice, and Ho (2001) described three possible approaches, drawing on the literature and their own experiences. First, some writers have suggested supervisors use semi-structured questions to begin the discussion (e.g., "What cultural variables construct your cultural identity?" "How do you feel about your client's race?" [p. 124]). Others support a mutual exchange regarding supervisor-supervisee differences and how these may affect their work together, as illustrated by this suggested statement in Hird et al.:

> An important component of my supervision model includes developing a trusting relationship with my supervisee. As we sit here, I notice that there are a lot of differences that exist between the two of us, such as gender, race and ethnicity, and age. I'm wondering how that might affect our ability to develop a strong working relationship. Let me tell you some of my thoughts. I'd also be interested in hearing yours as well. (p. 124)

Hird et al. also described a third, more personal approach. The example given involved a White male supervisor who self-disclosed his process of becoming aware of the importance of cultural variables in counseling and supervision, as well as recognition of his own White privilege experiences.

Over the years, we have tried various formats also, and watched our supervisors-in-training experiment with their own ideas. We have come to believe that each supervisor needs to find his or her own, individual way of introducing diversity issues into the supervision agenda, and have found that a supervisor's preferred way may change over time. An African-American male supervisor likely will have a somewhat different "lead-in" from a White female supervisor who is gay. Both might begin, however, with a statement such as the following: "I'm aware that I'm an African-American male and you [the supervisee] are a White female, and we both grew up in the South. I'm also aware that most of your clients will be White middle-class females. I'm wondering what your thoughts are about how diversity issues may be relevant to our work together." We have observed supervisees respond in a variety of ways to such statements, from telling part of their life history to describing previous interactions in a work environment. All of these responses are "correct" because the goal is to start the conversation about diversity issues. The message has been given: "It is okay and it is important that both of us feel free to bring up diversity issues concerning your clients *and us* during our supervision sessions."

As these examples hopefully suggest, the diversity variables relevant to supervision include not only race, ethnicity, and gender, but also sexual orientation, socioeconomic status, religious beliefs, geographical influences, disability issues, and any and all other cultural contexts for the supervisor, supervisee, and client, as well as the counseling and supervision settings. Which variables are introduced during the first supervision session is the supervisor's choice but should be the result of a deliberate decision based on the particular supervision context. It is not necessary (or sometimes even advisable) for a male supervisor who is gay to come out to every supervisee in the first session (or any subsequent session), and it is not intended that all supervisor-supervisee similarities and differences be identified in the first session (which would be impossible). Rather, the intention is to start a conversation that will enrich the supervisee's work with clients as well as the supervisory relationship.

Duan and Roehlke's (2001) results are important to keep in mind here. They found that supervisors believed their efforts to address cultural issues were greater than their supervisee perceptions of those efforts. In addition, the supervisees said they were more willing to self-disclose about cultural issues than their supervisors believed they were. So, your initial approach may not be as effective or heard as well as you think it was heard. And remember, this is an initial approach that begins a dialogue you as supervisor will need to nurture and continue to articulate.

Initial Assessment of the Supervisee

In all of these activities—establishing a contract, identifying learning goals, discussing expectations and hopes, introducing multicultural issues—the supervisor has the opportunity to make an initial assessment of the supervisee. Supervisees' responses to your multicultural and diversity statements give you an initial glimpse of their comfort level in discussing these issues, which issues are particularly salient to a supervisee, and, perhaps, some level of awareness regarding diversity dynamics in relationships. The presentation of self, from the first point of contact to the closing moment, provides some glimpses of how the supervisee approaches new relationships and learning contexts. Discussion of learning goals indicates what areas are important to the supervisee or which the supervisee is willing to put on the agenda.

The initial assessment will continue across several sessions. It takes some time to assess all areas of counselor growth and identify themes and patterns. With the first client or session tape, you can begin to assess the supervisee's skill level. Discussion of that client will offer an initial idea of how the supervisee conceptualizes a client. All of these discussions also will alert you to the supervisee's developmental level and needs. As suggested earlier, almost any supervisory intervention used in initial and subsequent sessions provides assessment information. In the next chapter, we describe several interventions you may use, as well as the factors involved in choosing which intervention to use.

Discussion Questions

1. Discuss with your colleagues the question posed early in this chapter: After the first session, how do you want the supervisee to describe his or her anticipations about working with you to a colleague and fellow student?
2. What information do you have about a new supervisee? How might that information interfere with your work with that supervisee?
3. What aspects of the supervisory contract are particularly important for your work setting?

4. Look back at the learning goals you wrote at the end of chapter 1. To what extent are they realistic, concrete, and specific?
5. You are supervising Janice (an African-American female, late forties, widowed, no children, living with her elderly mother) as she works toward her state certification in school counseling. Janice is an experienced middle-school teacher and a Licensed Professional Counselor (LPC) with Mental Health counseling experience. She is articulate and eager to learn, as well as very kind and understanding with the elementary school children who are her clients. Possibly due to her prior counseling experience, Janice demonstrates strong case conceptualization skills, but is somewhat weak with confronting her current clients. Because of her lifestyle, she knows very little about children's toys, movies, books, other interests, and this often affects her individual counseling sessions, leading to delayed trust building and rapport. Because it often takes her a while to understand what the younger children are talking about, she ends up asking too many questions to gather information. This keeps her from reflecting feelings or actually working on counseling goals, prolonging the counseling sessions unnecessarily.
   a. What is your assessment of Janice's current developmental level?
   b. How might her prior experience distort your perceptions of her current counseling abilities?
6. How will you introduce multicultural and diversity issues in the first session with your supervisee?

Chapter 3

Supervision Interventions

The *intentional* counseling supervisor makes deliberate choices about what interventions will be used in a supervisory session. These choices are made either consciously or subconsciously. The more conscious these choices are, the better, as conscious choices imply that the supervisor is aware of the factors influencing decisions, and can make sure all the relevant factors are considered in choosing an intervention.

Choosing Supervision Interventions

Supervisor Preferences

At the broadest levels, your intervention choices are influenced by your worldview and theoretical orientation to counseling (Friedlander & Ward, 1984). As noted in chapter 1 (this volume), your beliefs about why people behave the way they do, how change happens, and the relative role of cognitions, behaviors, and emotions in working with clients, as a few examples, necessarily influence decisions you make about supervision. Relatedly, your ideas about how people learn also are at work in your decisions. The clearer you can be about your own worldview and theoretical orientations—and the advantages and limitations of them—the more conscious you can be about your choices, including the situations in which they are more effective. Such awarenesses also, then, are a prerequisite for becoming more flexible in your supervision interventions.

Clearly, other factors also will influence your choices, including your personality characteristics (which probably are reflected in your broader beliefs also) as well as your own experiences as a supervisee and, if applicable, your experiences as a supervisor, teacher, and consultant. In particular, supervisors sometimes adopt a supervision stance that mirrors what worked best for them. Others are determined to do the opposite of what was done to them. Of course, awareness of these biases help the supervisor step back and make sure that these supervision preferences are really appropriate for a particular supervisee, in a particular supervisory session.

DOI: 10.4324/9781003251583-3

Importantly, one's worldview or assumptive world (Friedlander & Ward, 1984) also refers to one's cultural background and perspectives. Clearly, these beliefs, and one's personal and professional experiences with diversity, need to be revisited in preparation for discussing multicultural issues in the first supervision session (see chap. 2, this volume) as well as one's ongoing work with supervisees.

In our supervisor training experiences, we have found that every participant arrives with at least a few strong ideas—reflecting their broader beliefs—that influence their supervision intervention choices. In training groups or classes, this can become quite an advantage. For example, the more cognitively oriented supervisor knows who to call on in the group for helpful consultation about working with a supervisee who has difficulty exploring client emotions. The supervisor who so easily recognizes personal issues affecting a supervisee's work is a help to all, and can use the group members to make sure that efforts to address personal issues are developmentally appropriate and within ethical guidelines. The experienced teacher in the group knows how to break down complex clinical interventions into manageable, sequential steps that can be explained in language familiar to the novice. In short, each supervisor brings valuable skills and perspectives that can be shared with colleagues, as well as the need to identify limitations of these perspectives and preferences, gain appreciation for other perspectives, and meet the challenge of expanding the repertoire of available supervision interventions.

Beyond general exploration and discussion of your worldviews, theoretical orientations, and beliefs and preferences, you also can use several structured exercises that operationalize some of your preferences. Bernard (Bernard & Goodyear, 1998), for example, suggested an activity in which a supervisor audiotapes a role-play of a supervision session; the audiotape is then analyzed to determine the primary role (e.g., teacher, counselor, consultant) portrayed by the supervisor. Importantly, Bernard noted that supervisors often are surprised by their results. Like Bernard, we have found the most common dissonance to be a supervisor who states a preference for the counselor role, but who behaves much more in a teacher role. Even Carl Rogers apparently experienced this dissonance, per his discussion of his supervision work with Hackney and Goodyear (1984). Perhaps some counselors want to avoid the more directive behaviors typically associated with the teacher role (which means they misunderstand the teacher role), and thus prefer to see themselves in the counselor role. At any rate, it seems that review of a practice supervision session might best involve both self-evaluation and review by others.

Several more objective measures also can be used to identify your preferences. The Supervisor Emphasis Rating Form-Revised (SERF-R; Lanning & Freeman, 1994; Table 3.1) challenges supervisors to prioritize four areas of emphasis that are based in and expand the focus areas in the discrimination model (Bernard, 1979, 1997). The SERF-R yields a rank ordering of the degree to which one emphasizes counseling performance skills, cognitive counseling

Table 3.1 Supervisor Emphasis Rating Form—Revised

Directions: A number of competencies that many supervisors consider important for counselors to demonstrate in practicum are listed below. Competencies are listed in sets of four. You are requested to rank order the competencies in each set from 1 to 4 in terms of how likely you are to emphasize each in supervision with a beginning master's student. Within each set, please rank the one you would *most likely emphasize* as "1" and the one you would *least likely emphasize* as "4." Please rank *all* the competencies within all sets.

1. _____ A. The counselor maintains appropriate conduct in personal relationships with clients.
   _____ B. The counselor uses appropriate reflection of feeling with client.
   _____ C. The counselor maintains a non-judgmental attitude despite value differences with a client.
   _____ D. The counselor is able to prioritize client problems.
2. _____ A. The counselor is knowledgeable about ethical codes of behavior.
   _____ B. The counselor is able to identify client themes.
   _____ C. The counselor recognizes his/her personal limitations and strengths.
   _____ D. The counselor demonstrates the use of open-ended questions.
3. _____ A. The counselor is aware of socioeconomic and/or cultural factors that may influence the counseling session.
   _____ B. The counselor uses open-ended questions and allows the client maximum freedom of expression.
   _____ C. The counselor is aware of his/her own needs and conflicts.
   _____ D. The counselor keeps appointments with clients.
4. _____ A. The counselor makes appropriate use of additional information obtained from other professional sources.
   _____ B. The counselor is able to risk self in counseling with a client.
   _____ C. The counselor communicates his/her sincerity and genuineness to the client.
   _____ D. The counselor maintains confidentiality of client information.
5. _____ A. The counselor is aware of the effects of his/her own anxiety in the counseling process.
   _____ B. The counselor engages in appropriate confrontation with the client.
   _____ C. The counselor recognizes when he/she needs consultative help from another professional.
   _____ D. The counselor is able to set attainable goals in line with client readiness.
6. _____ A. The counselor shows a commitment to personal growth.
   _____ B. The counselor prepares clients for termination.
   _____ C. The counselor responds to client non-verbal behavior.
   _____ D. The counselor understands how people are the same even though they may be worked with differently.
7. _____ A. The counselor is able to develop short and long term goals with a client.
   _____ B. The counselor allows him/herself the freedom to be wrong in the counseling session.

(*Continued*)

Table 3.1 (Continued)

_____ C. The counselor communicates his/her respect and positive regard to the client.
_____ D. The counselor actively participates in professional organizations.
8. _____ A. The counselor formulates specific plans and strategies for client behavior change.
_____ B. The counselor makes appropriate referrals of clients.
_____ C. The counselor is able to keep personal problems out of the counseling session.
_____ D. The counselor accurately reflects the content of a client's speech.
9. _____ A. The counselor is able to manage a strong expression of client's feelings.
_____ B. The counselor is on time for client appointments.
_____ C. The counselor receives feedback in a non-defensive fashion.
_____ D. The counselor is aware of the client's potential for successful counseling progress.
10. _____ A. The counselor recognizes when a client needs help in continuing to cope.
_____ B. The counselor takes advantage of opportunities for additional training.
_____ C. The counselor is able to identify and manage personal feelings that are generated in counseling.
_____ D. The counselor maintains a receptive and appropriate posture during the session.
11. _____ A. The counselor recognizes and admits when he/she enters into a "power struggle" with the clients.
_____ B. The counselor appropriately summarizes client statements.
_____ C. The counselor dresses appropriately.
_____ D. The counselor conceptualizes a client accurately within a theoretical frame of reference.
12. _____ A. The counselor identifies the need for and uses immediacy appropriately.
_____ B. The counselor engages in adequate note-keeping on clients.
_____ C. The counselor is able to choose and apply techniques appropriately.
_____ D. The counselor is able to tolerate ambiguity in the counseling sessions.
13. _____ A. The counselor maintains appropriate relationships with professional colleagues.
_____ B. The counselor is able to interpret client behaviors within a coherent theoretical framework.
C. The counselor can effectively manage his/her frustration with lack of progress with clients.
D. The counselor engages in appropriate nonverbal expressions.
14. _____ A. The counselor exhibits appropriate eye contact.
_____ B. The counselor understands which techniques are compatible and consistent with his/her stated theoretical model.

_____ C. The counselor is aware of his/her personal needs for approval from the client.

_____ D. The counselor engages in adequate preparation for counseling sessions.

15. _____ A. The counselor is aware of how his/her attraction to the client is affecting the counseling process.

_____ B. The counselor maintains her/his office neatly and orderly.

_____ C. The counselor reinforces appropriate client behavior.

_____ D. The counselor is able to predict the effects on a client of the techniques applied in counseling.

Developed by W. Lanning & Associates (Lanning, 1986; Lanning & Freeman, 1994).

skills, self-awareness, and professional behaviors (our adapted terms) during supervision sessions. The Supervisory Styles Inventory (SSI; Friedlander & Ward, 1984; Table 3.2) measures self-ratings of three styles that easily translate into the three supervisory roles: task-oriented (teacher), interpersonally sensitive (counselor), and attractive (consultant). These measures can be completed in regards to your ideal preferences, your current supervision work, or how you believe you will behave (or should behave) in an upcoming supervision experience with a particular supervisee (e.g., a novice vs. a developmentally advanced supervisee).

Beyond these more supervisor-based factors, there are other important considerations that need to be a part of your decision-making process. These additional factors include the following: (a) the developmental level of your supervisee; (b) your supervisee's stated learning goals; (c) your own goals for the supervisee; (d) your own learning goals for your supervision work with this supervisee; and (e) contextual factors, such as the counseling setting, course requirements or licensure regulations, other supervisors or administrators who will have some oversight with the supervisee, timeframe for this supervision experience, and so forth.

Supervisee Developmental Level

Developmental models and stages of counselor development were described in chapter 1 (this volume). As indicated earlier, the optimal environment (Stoltenberg, 1981) to encourage counselor growth varies by developmental level, and requires intentional and proactive planning by the supervisor. At beginning levels, the need to take more of a teacher role will be clear. These supervisees often arrive with a long list of specific questions, primarily concerning which technique to use with a particular client or "how to" questions about employing a particular skill. Supervision sessions typically are very detail oriented and mostly skill based. Thus, supervisors of supervisees at early developmental levels often employ instructional and experiential

Table 3.2 Supervisory Styles Inventory

Please indicate your perception of your style as a supervisor of counselors on each of the following descriptors. Circle the number on the scale, from 1 to 7, which best reflects your view of yourself.

	not very						*very*
1. goal-oriented	1	2	3	4	5	6	7
2. perceptive	1	2	3	4	5	6	7
3. concrete	1	2	3	4	5	6	7
4. explicit	1	2	3	4	5	6	7
5. committed	1	2	3	4	5	6	7
6. affirming	1	2	3	4	5	6	7
7. practical	1	2	3	4	5	6	7
8. sensitive	1	2	3	4	5	6	7
9. collaborative	1	2	3	4	5	6	7
10. intuitive	1	2	3	4	5	6	7
11. reflective	1	2	3	4	5	6	7
12. responsive	1	2	3	4	5	6	7
13. structured	1	2	3	4	5	6	7
14. evaluative	1	2	3	4	5	6	7
15. friendly	1	2	3	4	5	6	7
16. flexible	1	2	3	4	5	6	7
17. prescriptive	1	2	3	4	5	6	7
18. didactic	1	2	3	4	5	6	7
19. thorough	1	2	3	4	5	6	7
20. focused	1	2	3	4	5	6	7
21. creative	1	2	3	4	5	6	7
22. supportive	1	2	3	4	5	6	7
23. open	1	2	3	4	5	6	7
24. realistic	1	2	3	4	5	6	7
25. resourceful	1	2	3	4	5	6	7
26. invested	1	2	3	4	5	6	7
27. facilitative	1	2	3	4	5	6	7
28. therapeutic	1	2	3	4	5	6	7
29. positive	1	2	3	4	5	6	7
30. trusting	1	2	3	4	5	6	7
31. informative	1	2	3	4	5	6	7
32. humorous	1	2	3	4	5	6	7
33. warm	1	2	3	4	5	6	7

Developed by M. L. Friedlander & L. G. Ward (1984). Unpublished instrument.

interventions such as demonstrating and modeling, role-playing, explaining, and providing resources (e.g., readings; Rønnestad & Skovholt, 1993; Stoltenberg, 1981). For example, at the first author's university, supervisors of novice counselors working with children often schedule their supervision sessions in the play therapy room where they can quickly demonstrate or role-play a particular play therapy intervention. At the same time, a good measure of encouragement and support must be provided, given the high level of anxiety characteristic of beginning supervisees. Live observation may be welcomed—if not requested.

The middle developmental levels seem to correspond with the characteristics of graduate students nearing the end of their training and internship experiences. These supervisees still have lots of questions, but they are more likely to investigate clinical options themselves (having learned how to access such resources from you previously). They even may share their assessments of the advantages and limitations of a technique with you, as well as their level of comfort with each. Your role, then, shifts to a more facilitative one, encouraging a thorough, open analysis of clinical options, what Rønnestad and Skovholt (1993) termed "clarifying feedback" (p. 401). Your instructional role now is focused on helping the supervisees fine-tune their performance, particularly in terms of how an intervention or technique needs to be adjusted or modified for a particular client, situation, or clinical goal. Remember, it's a good sign when a supervisee at this developmental level disagrees with your opinion of what to do with a client!

At the middle developmental levels, you will find your counseling skills to be quite useful, as your supervisees are becoming more aware of their reactions to clients as well as the potential clinical value of their reactions. Supervision interventions such as Interpersonal Process Recall (Kagan, 1980), metaphor (Young & Borders, 1998, 1999), and reflection (Neufeldt et al., 1995) are helpful in facilitating your supervisees' growth in this area. Your confrontation skills—as well as your methods for encouraging self-confrontation—also are quite appropriate and needed as supervisees try to deal productively with transference and countertransference issues. Use of your immediacy skills will highlight the processes at work in the counseling and supervision sessions, thus both facilitating the supervision *and* modeling this intervention.

At the later developmental levels, you will be called on to be more of a consultant with your supervisees. These supervisees most often will be able to identify the needed focus for supervision and will request your help with more subtle or sophisticated issues, such as understanding an impasse, a confusing paradox, or an unexpected internal response to a client. There also may be issues related to the supervisee's evolving professional identity. As counselors age and face new developmental life tasks (e.g., middle-age concern for generativity), they have new questions, challenges, and priorities that must be considered and integrated into their counselor identity. Clearly, a number of your skills will be relevant at this stage. A major defining characteristic of your role at this level is the collegial, peer interaction. You will learn much from your supervisee at this level.

As a reminder, developmental level and experience level are not synonymous. Counselors with some years of experience may be functioning at middle—or early—developmental levels, particularly if they have not had counseling supervision since completing their internship. These counselors may have a limited repertoire of counseling skills and self-awareness, and struggle with conceptual questions and confusion.

Supervisees' Learning Goals

We discussed earlier (chap. 2, this volume) the merits of asking supervisees to identify several concrete goals, and offered several formats for writing relevant goals. We also offered some specifics regarding how you can use these goals in supervision. Clearly, supervision interventions should be chosen with some thought to helping supervisees work toward their own learning goals. You might even make the connection obvious to the supervisee: "Would you be willing to try a role-play? I think it would be a good way to work on your goal of using more open-ended questions." Or, "There is a supervision technique called IPR that was designed to help supervisees develop awareness of their reactions to clients, which is one of your learning goals. I wondered if you would work with me today in an IRP exercise with the videotape of your last session?"

In relation to their overall learning goals, supervisees typically are asked to identify specific questions for a particular client or counseling session to be discussed in supervision. These more focused questions usually reflect their larger learning goals (even if these goals have not yet been stated formally) and also will point toward appropriate supervision interventions.

Your Goals for the Supervisee

As suggested in chapter 2 (this volume), your goals for the supervisee—goals the supervisee cannot or does not identify—emerge from your ongoing assessment of the supervisee. This assessment is about much more than skill proficiency. The supervisor also will observe which counseling skills are used and which are not evident, session pacing, the supervisee's comfort level with various clinical topics and clients, openness to supervisory feedback, interactions with peers during group supervision sessions, anxiety level and when anxiety increases and decreases, as well as the supervisee's methods for dealing with anxiety, and so forth—all of which may need to become a focus of supervisory interventions. Within a university setting, we have found that it takes about one third of a semester for these issues to emerge. By this time, we have direct knowledge of the supervisee's work, as well as observations from our interactions with the student in supervision sessions, so that themes and patterns have begun to emerge. Whether your goals are ever shared with your supervisee, they necessarily will guide your selection of supervision interventions.

Your Own Learning Goals as a Supervisor

It is certainly appropriate to base some supervision intervention choices in your own learning goals and professional development. You may be ready to try a new intervention in individual or group supervision; want to develop greater skill and confidence in the teacher, counselor, or consultant role; or work toward greater comfort with confronting supervisees. Although client and supervisee needs take priority, it is likely that your goals and their needs often will be an appropriate match.

Contextual Factors

Does your facility have a one-way mirror and observation deck for live observation? Do you have telephone equipment to allow contact with the supervisee during a session (live supervision)? Is videotaping possible? Obviously, the physical setting will affect your choice of supervision interventions—although supervisors often become creative when they believe a particular intervention is needed. In addition, site policies also may affect your supervisory work, such as limits on the number of counseling sessions per client, an emphasis on psychoeducational group approaches versus individual clinical approaches, or discouragement of discussing some topics with school-based student clients. In some states, licensure regulations require that direct observation supervisory methods be used with licensure applicants (Borders & Cashwell, 1992; Borders, Cashwell, & Rotter, 1995). You also may be working collaboratively with an onsite clinical or administrative supervisor who has additional requirements, preferences, and responsibilities related to oversight of the supervisee's work.

What is the purpose of your supervision? Are you charged with skill development primarily? Are you evaluating whether this person is ready to be licensed? Are you being asked to help with a subgroup of a supervisee's clients because of your clinical expertise? What degree of client protection is needed? What is the match or mismatch of supervisee skill level and level of client difficulty? (Goodyear & Nelson, 1997). Supervisors should be clear concerning their purpose and tasks, and, assuming they agree to these tasks, choose supervision interventions that are an appropriate match.

Planning for a Supervision Session

In a typical scenario, you receive an audiotape or videotape of a counseling session and the supervisee's self-evaluation of the session several days before the supervision session is scheduled. As requested, your supervisee's self-evaluation includes information relevant to your planning and your choice of interventions. You know what the supervisee hoped to accomplish in the session with this client as well as his or her self-assessment of how well these plans unfolded (or didn't happen) in the session, and specific questions and needs for supervision. You read this tape critique carefully, noting the supervisee's specific requests for supervision in particular. Then you settle in for your own review of the tape, taking notes on the content, identifying statements or portions of the tape that are particularly relevant to the counselor's stated needs and overall learning goals, jotting down observations or questions about the counselor more so than the client (Borders, 1992). At the end, you review your notes for themes and patterns, and, as needed, determine priorities. You know that realistically your supervisee can hear a maximum of three points during a supervision session, so you take care to make good choices, with at least one point having relevance to the supervisee's learning goals. Importantly, these points are stated as *supervision goals*—what the supervisee will gain from attention to these points—rather than *agenda items*—things you will do in the session. Why you are doing what you are doing addresses the goal of your action. This difference may seem subtle or trivial, but attention to goals helps make sure you focus on the supervisee's learning and not just the method. The method, or intervention, should follow the goal (i.e., why you choose a particular method). Then, you consider which supervisory interventions are appropriate to your three (or two or one) supervision goals, and which also match the other factors that influence your choice (e.g., counselor developmental level and motivational style, the supervision facility, your goal to use more experiential supervision interventions, etc.), and you make a plan.

At this point you know what you want to cover, and you have a pretty good idea of how you want to approach each point. You also are aware that the supervisee may arrive with additional needs, and that some parts of your plan may take more or less time than you anticipated. So, you consider, of your plans, which points can wait and which must be addressed. Your planning is intentional and proactive as well as flexible.

You probably have noticed that you have read a good portion of this book and you still haven't read about how to conduct a supervision session, except the initial one. This is intentional—and appropriate. To be an effective supervisor, you will spend at least as much time in preparing for a session as you spend conducting or facilitating the actual session. Supervision sessions do not begin with your asking the supervisee, "What would you like to do today?" Instead, you likely share your agenda and sessions goals, in the supervisee's language, ask if the supervisee has other issues that need to be addressed, and make any needed adjustments to your plan. This "business" of the session is conducted, of course, in a warm and supportive manner that contributes to the other message you are delivering: that supervision of this supervisee is important to you, that you've spent some time preparing so as to be as helpful as you can be in this supervisee's growth and development, you want to hear any other concerns, and you are ready to work! These messages are good models for supervisees' approach to counseling sessions as well as their preparation for supervision sessions.

Implementing Supervision Interventions

Our biases will become clear in this overview of supervision interventions—and likely will be no surprise to you. Our preferences for direct observation of a supervisee's work and interventions based in educational principles also are not unique. We would add that we also believe that there is no bad intervention per se. Each intervention has its advantages and limitations, each has its purpose. Our emphasis—again, no surprise—is on encouraging supervisors to be clear about the purpose(s), so that an informed choice of an intervention(s)—one that fits your goals for a particular session—is possible. As stated earlier, each intervention can be used as an assessment of the supervisee, an intervention meant to facilitate change, and an evaluation of progress (Borders et al., 1991), sometimes simultaneously. These different uses are illustrated later.

In the following section, our goal is to provide a brief introduction and overview of the most commonly used supervision interventions in individual supervision sessions (group supervision is covered in chap. 4, this volume). There are many variations on each intervention. Some variations have been published, sometimes labeled with clever acronyms, so that you can read and determine which variations are appropriate to your own supervision work or get some sense of how to adapt these yourself for your work, your style, and your supervisees. Our favorite sources for descriptions of supervision interventions are *Counselor Education and Supervision*, the journal published by the Association for Counselor Education and Supervision, *The Clinical Supervisor*, a multidisciplinary journal, and each edition of Bernard and Goodyear's (1992, 1998, 2004) text, *Fundamentals of Clinical Supervision.*

Self-Report

Self-report is both the most commonly used intervention (Borders & Usher, 1992; Goodyear & Nelson, 1997; Roberts & Borders, 1994)—likely due to its convenience—and the most criticized intervention. Essentially, self-report means the supervisee makes a verbal report of what happened in one or more sessions with a client. Limitations of this approach are obvious. The supervisee can only report what he or she consciously heard and observed, through whatever biases and unconscious filters govern the supervisee's conscious awareness. In addition, the supervisee intentionally can choose what to report and not report, as well as what to emphasize or de-emphasize, and so forth. Critical information about the client (or couple or family or group) or the counseling relationship may be left out, consciously or unconsciously.

These same factors, however, highlight the usefulness of this approach, particularly as an adjunct to other supervisory interventions. Over time, a supervisee's self-reports reveal what information is apparently outside the supervisee's awareness. Patterns and themes of omissions become evident. These omissions may become the focus of other interventions, such as having the supervisee watch a videotape without sound to force a focus on nonverbal behaviors, or confronting the discrepancy between the self-report and session content (per supervisor's review of session audiotape). In addition, how the supervisee self-reports may be "the message," particularly if the supervisee behaves differently, becomes animated or flat. This self-report could be the supervisee's unconscious attempt to play the role of the client, the first step in a parallel process (Goodyear & Nelson, 1997; Levenson, 1984; see also chap. 5, this volume, for a discussion of parallel process) that may become the focus of supervision.

It is likely that self-report is more reliable with supervisees at more advanced developmental levels, as they have achieved a certain measure of self-awareness as well as recognition of the key issues that need to be reported, and may be less likely to self-protect in their verbal reports. Nevertheless, self-reports at beginning levels are instructive, and changes in self-reports (e.g., fewer omissions, more awareness) can be useful in evaluating supervisee progress.

Process Notes

Process notes are distinct from case notes. The latter are a report of the session content, including the client's report, the identified problems, and the counseling interventions used. In contrast, process notes are the supervisee's reflections on the processes of the client, the counselor, their interactions and relationship. To be effective, at least in early use of this approach, supervisors need to provide a structure or format that encourages introspection and reflection.

Typically, these formats include questions focused on the counselor's feelings and thoughts about the client; rationale for interventions used in the session; preferred and alternative hypotheses about the client, client–counselor interactions, and session content and flow; attention to potential diversity issues; and perhaps some IPR-type questions concerning the client's thoughts and feelings about the counselor (Bernard & Goodyear, 1998; Goldberg, 1985; Goodyear & Nelson, 1997).

Much like self-report, process notes likely are limited by supervisee awareness and developmental level. Although advanced supervisees' process notes may be richer, a beginning supervisee's use of this approach (perhaps with a limited focus on one or two process questions) can help that supervisee start developing an awareness of process elements and an appreciation for their value in understanding a client and the work of a counselor. Process notes also provide an assessment of current awareness of feelings and cognitions, and a measure of improved awareness over time. Likely, as with self-report, the use of process notes in conjunction with other supervision interventions is preferred. For example, process notes for a session could be part of the tape critique turned in with a session audiotape. The supervisor's review of both the notes and the tape can yield rich material for the supervision session.

Audiotapes and Videotapes

Rogers (1942; Goodyear & Nelson, 1997) was one of the first to advocate for the use of electrically recorded interviews in counselor training and supervision. Today, use of audiotapes and videotapes are common and valued modes of supervision, with increasing ease of use due to technological developments. Most basically, tapes provide access to the actual counseling session content, and so are an important complement—and contrast—to self-reports and process notes. Having tapes available, however, does not ensure quality supervision.

As with other supervisory interventions, the particular method of tape review should be grounded in a supervisee's learning goals and the supervisor's session goals. Often, these goals are reflected in a required self-review and tape critique that is turned in to the supervisor along with the tape. The tape-critique format may be some combination of case notes, process notes, and self-evaluation, or emphasize only one of these, based on the instruction or processes desired through this method. Regardless of format, a supervisee's self-review—structured by the tape-critique format—is a critical component. Supervisees' review of their own tapes of counseling sessions is a teaching tool. For example, focused observations via tape review increase awareness that can lead to greater in-session awareness, a better appreciation of one's strengths and areas for growth, and more accurate self-monitoring and self-supervision.

For the most part, we suggest that supervisors review the entire tape. Otherwise, the supervisor may make observations and suggestions that were used in nonreviewed portions of the session, or that even are inappropriate based on information revealed in those portions. In addition, the supervisor is not able to assess counselor pacing of the session, as well as the flow and process dynamics, and the supervisor may miss problems—or strengths—in how a supervisee opens or closes a session. Reviewing entire sessions seems particularly critical for supervisors in university training programs, as they are working with beginning-level counselors who need lots of feedback, and they will need to certify that these supervisees have sufficient entry-level skills to graduate. In fact, internship supervision may be the last supervision some counselors receive, particularly school counselors, who also may be the only counselor in their work setting. Even counselors who seek licensure may find their postdegree supervision to be less intense and more irregular, less focused on their professional development and more like case staffing than supervision. As our interns near the end of their academic training and they realize the likely realities of postdegree supervision, we often hear comments and questions such as "May I call you if I get stuck?" and "What do I do if I get a client with an issue that I've never worked with before?" For these counselors-in-training, then, review of entire tapes—the relatively few we can hear across two semesters of supervision—seems an ethical imperative. Even so, we have found this practice also to be a sound one with experienced doctoral students and other advanced supervisees. Typically, these persons have returned to supervision with specific goals for enhancing and broadening their work, a few blind spots, and a couple of bad habits. Review of entire tapes is necessary to attend to these needs.

That said, there certainly are situations and supervisees where a different approach is appropriate, perhaps at least as a change of pace. In these cases, supervisors could ask supervisees to select a segment of tape for review. Regardless the amount of review, a supervisor can still request that the counselor identify segments of tape for focused review, providing an instructive guide for the supervisee and a focus for supervision. Perhaps most often the supervisor—directly or indirectly—asks supervisees to identify a segment that illustrates their struggle with the client or session—in other words, the place where they most need help. Preselected segments, however, can be tailored to the supervisee's learning goals, such as identifying one to three times when the supervisee believes a confrontation was needed. In this case, supervision can be skill oriented (practicing confrontive statements that would have been appropriate) and address conceptual and self-awareness issues (what kept the supervisee from making a confrontive statement: client dynamics? supervisee fears?). There also needs to be a balance of problem areas and strengths. Supervisees should be encouraged—if not required—to present at least one session tape that shows their best work, a session they are especially proud of, or one in which they at least partially achieved a performance goal. For our university supervisees, we also want to review a variety of counseling work—difficult clients and clients making progress; clients with a variety of clinical issues; individual, group, and, if available, family and couple sessions; intakes, middle sessions, and termination sessions.

Among the structured approaches to review of tapes, the most well-known are microtraining (Daniels, Rigazio-Digilio, & Ivey, 1997; Forsyth & Ivey, 1980) and Interpersonal Process Recall (Kagan, 1980; Kagan & Kagan, 1997). Both approaches have been found effective in a number of studies, and the two have very different purposes and goals.

Microtraining

Microtraining is most appropriate for skill acquisition. Originally designed to teach basic helping skills, more advanced skills have been added to the program. In fact, Ivey's (1994; Daniels et al., 1997) microskills hierarchy ranges from attending behaviors to skill integration and developing one's own style and theory. In addition, Greenberg (1980) developed a microtraining-type approach for teaching gestalt techniques. Microtraining follows a step-by-step procedure: (a) Skills or parts of skills or techniques are isolated and taught one at a time; (b) the skill is explained via lecture and written materials, and, most importantly, is modeled; (c) the supervisee practices the skill and receives feedback via self-observation of audiotapes and videotapes as well as from peers, trainees, and supervisors. There is ample empirical support for the effectiveness of microtraining. Research evidence also indicates that, with follow-up training and reinforcement, counselors transfer learning to actual counseling sessions. Micro training may be most useful with a supervisee who has a specific skill deficit but also may be seen—at least in adapted form—through role-plays in supervision.

Interpersonal Process Recall

In contrast to microtraining's focus on skill development, *Interpersonal Process Recall* (IPR; Kagan, 1980; Kagan & Kagan, 1997) was designed to increase self-awareness, particularly counselors' in-session thoughts and feelings. It is assumed that there are perceptions kept just beyond the counselors' self-awareness as a self-protection. Allowing these perceptions into consciousness awareness would threaten the counselor's sense of psychology safety in interpersonal exchanges. Based in humanistic and phenomenological theories, IPR is designed to provide the optimal environment to allow counselors to become aware of these covert thoughts and feelings, and feel free to express these in the here-and-now without experiencing the anticipated negative consequences. As a result, counselors discover those instances in which they fail to deal with clients' covert messages as well as their own reactions to these messages. IPR allows counselors to practice using facilitation and confrontation skills, based in their increased awareness, and thus encourages a deeper level of involvement with their clients.

Following the steps of IPR, a supervisor and counselor review a counseling session tape, or portion of a tape, together. Either person can stop the tape at any time, giving the counselor the opportunity to say aloud what he or she was thinking and feeling at that time, as if the counselor is back in that moment (vs. evaluative statements or any commentary about what happened then). In essence, the counselor is invited to re-experience the counseling session without the distractions and pressures of being with the client. In fact, we suggest the recall be expressed in the present tense as a way of helping the counselor really be present in the actual here-and-now of the session.

To encourage in-depth recall, the supervisor takes on the nonevaluative role of an inquirer. To create and maintain the necessary environment, the supervisor must remain in that role until the IPR process is completed or ended. As suggested by the term *inquirer*, the supervisor asks questions to broaden and enhance the counselor's recall of in-session thoughts and feelings, such as "What were you thinking just then?," "How did you want the client to perceive you?," "Was there anything that you wanted to say but didn't say at that time?," "What kept you from sharing that?," "What do you think the client wanted from you at that moment?," and "Do you think the client was aware of your feelings about her at that moment?" The supervisor also asks follow-up probes to encourage further reflection (e.g., "What effect did that perception have on you?"). (A more complete listing of inquirer questions can be found in Bernard & Goodyear, 1998, and Kagan, 1975.) As an inquirer, the supervisor helps the counselor stay in the recall mode (vs. self-evaluation or conceptualizing about the client, etc.).

It is particularly important that the supervisor maintain a nonjudgmental stance and be accepting of negative feelings, including any negative thoughts and feelings about the client. As Kagan (1975) emphasized, the supervisor is to listen and learn—not teach. This is not as simple as it sounds (Cashwell, 1994). Without realizing it, supervisors easily slip into asking questions such as "Were you aware of the client's tears?" that, at the least, have an indirect or implied evaluative tone. Such questions are outside the inquirer role, leading counselors to explain or even defend their in-session awareness and behaviors versus freely sharing what was going on for them at that moment. Even in the followup processing, the supervisor inquires of the counselor what he or she learned or became aware of during the IPR session. As the counselor processes the experience, the supervisor remains nonjudgmental, and summarizes rather than interprets.

Given the rather dramatic role change for the supervisor during IPR, it is important that the purpose of the procedure be explained to the supervisee, including how the approach may facilitate growth along the supervisee's learning goals. In addition, the existence of covert thoughts and feelings should be normalized as a way of attending to supervisee anxiety. Kagan (1975) suggested the supervisor/inquirer introduce IPR with statements such as the following:

> It's clear our mind works faster than our voice during a session, so that there were things you were vaguely aware of but didn't have time to put words to it, or you weren't sure these were things you should share with the client. And even if you did have the awareness at the moment, there's just not enough time to say everything in your head. You may have impressions of the client, or ideas about the client's impressions of you. Sometimes during a session, images come to mind or we have body reactions to a client or something a client says. Our goal today is to bring these thoughts, feelings, impressions, images, and reactions into conscious awareness and see what we can learn from them.

These statements are similar to guidelines suggested for setting up gestalt exercises with clients, and your knowledge and experience with such techniques can be helpful here.

Statements that help the counselor become aware of sensory experiences during the session may enhance the recall, and inviting the counselor to participate in the experiment may encourage greater disclosure. For example, a lead-in to help the counselor get back to that time and place is useful, such as:

> So, to try to get back to your awarenesses during that session, try to remember what you were thinking about just before the session began, how the client reacted when you greeted her in the waiting room, and your initial thoughts or impressions as you entered the counseling room

and started the session. Is some of that coming back to you? Okay, do you think we can begin?

Similarly, we find that inviting the counselor to try the IPR approach (as a way of addressing one of their learning goals or questions about the session) helps create a more positive set and openness to the experience. We've never gotten a "no" response; we have gotten expressions of reluctance, which typically has meant some part of the approach needs to be explained further or better.

IPR also can be applied in a client recall session and a mutual recall process involving both the counselor and client. The procedure (i.e., reviewing tape, inquirer role, and questions) are the same, adapted for the new recall participants. Here, of course, the purposes are different. From a supervisor perspective, client recall offers a check on the counselor's perceptions as well as feedback on effectiveness. For instance, we have heard a client reveal (knowing his counselor was behind the one-way mirror observing the recall session conducted by the supervisor) that "I knew what he wanted me to say and so that's what I said, but it's not at all what I plan to do." Blocher (1983) stated that one characteristic of a highly functioning counselor is the ability to recognize client feedback in session, and client recall can foster greater recognition of such feedback.

Mutual recall encourages counselor-client discourse at a different level. In fact, a supervisor may choose mutual recall as an intervention to change the way the counselor and client are communicating. Now, after asking the counselor, "What do you think the client wanted from you just then?," the supervisor can ask the client, "Were you aware that the counselor had this perception of you?" Mutual recall is particularly effective in dealing with interpersonal dynamics in counseling. For us, mutual recall is always a preferred option when we are stumped by an impasse in the counselor-client relationship. Often, the block that surfaces through the process was an unknown issue, at least at the conscious level. Sometimes, the interference was a dynamic in the counselor's life that was being played out in the counseling session but really had nothing to do with the client. In short, be open to what may be revealed via mutual recall (and other recall sessions). Beginning with assumptions about what will be revealed may hamper the process.

IPR can be slow (Bernard, 1989), depending on the length of tape reviewed and the extent of questions and recall. We know one supervisor who set aside 2 hours for any recall session. It is not necessary, however, to review the entire session. In fact, carefully selected sections, which lend themselves well to the purposes and goals of IPR, may be preferred. A session that combines IPR with another intervention may be needed. In the latter case, supervisors would need to clearly set forth their change in roles (e.g., inquirer) and concretely note the change for the supervisee.

For those new to IPR, we suggest practicing in a group. Supervisors in the group can indicate when they would like to stop the tape and ask a question.

Group members can help evaluate both the appropriateness and timing of the question as well as the wording of the question itself (i.e., inquirer vs. evaluative phrasing). Another constructive learning approach is to experience IPR as a participant. In fact, supervisor recall can provide constructive insights about the supervision relationship and other dynamics, much like counselor recall. We even have found supervisor-supervisee mutual recall helpful in breaking through a relationship impasse. The main caution, other than time requirements, is the possibility that interpersonal dynamics will be distorted or magnified out of proportion with such focused and intense scrutiny (Bernard, 1989).

Role-Plays

Role-plays are a very versatile supervision intervention, as they can be used for several different purposes and goals, including practicing skills and exploring client dynamics. Perhaps the more typical role-play scenario involves the supervisee in the counselor role and the supervisor in the client role, with the supervisee working on a particular skill deficit or learning and practicing a new technique. An advantage here is that supervisees can receive immediate feedback, and they can practice skills and techniques until they feel ready to use them with clients. Similarly, role-plays can be designed for practice responding to different types of clients (e.g., resistant, angry, dependent, suicidal, or seductive clients) that supervisees may encounter in a particular setting. Role-plays focused on skill development also may involve supervisor modeling of the skill or technique.

Beyond skills, role-plays also can be quite instructive about client dynamics and relationship issues. Variations of role-playing may be especially helpful for the counselor who reports client resistance or is having difficulty relating to the client effectively (Strosahl & Jacobson, 1986). For example, a supervisor may ask the supervisee to role-play the client—essentially, to "walk in the client's shoes"—as a way of better understanding the client's motivations, fears, intentions, or frame of reference. It may be that the supervisor perceives that the supervisee lacks empathy with a client and chooses this approach so that the supervisee can experience the client's frame of reference. It may be that the supervisor is unclear what dynamics are at work in the counseling session, and chooses a role-play as a way to try to achieve needed insights. In fact, the supervisor may take on the client role to better understand the client's perspective.

Although role-plays can be very helpful in clarifying client and relationship issues, the supervisor does need to be alert to the possibility that supervisees may inject some of their own dynamics into the role-play of the client, and attend to this as needed. Clearly, role-plays have multiple possibilities so that a key is to be aware of your purpose and goals in designing the role-play and assigning roles.

Modeling

Modeling, a component of microtraining, is perhaps most frequently associated with skill development, and it is certainly an effective approach, especially when it is combined with guided rehearsal and focused feedback (Akamatsu, 1980; Hosford & Barmann, 1983). Supervisors may model a variety of specific skills, opening or closing a session, or follow-up processing of an experiential exercise. One caution is that supervisees may be overwhelmed by a supervisor's skill level in role-playing the counselor so that one should model at a level that the supervisee can understand and achieve.

Modeling also has broader implications for supervisors who, in essence, are serving as an overt and subtle model during every moment of interaction with the supervisee. Perhaps most obviously, you are modeling counseling skills when you help the supervisee establish goals, reward risk taking, challenge and confront, and point out progress, as these are actions the supervisee also employs in counseling sessions. You also are constantly modeling professional and ethical behavior (i.e., how you handle confidentiality, your openness to feedback). Even more important, however, is the way you interact with the supervisee—your respect for and appreciation of the supervisee as a person. Similarly, your attitude about a client can speak volumes—and may be enacted by the supervisee in the next counseling session. Bottom line, be aware that your supervisees are watching and experiencing you, as a model, at all times (Borders, 2001).

Live Observation and Live Supervision

Many university settings, and some practice settings, have facilities that allow live observation and live supervision, including one-way mirrors and phone systems. Both involve direct observation of counseling sessions, with the key differentiation being whether there is interaction with the counselor during the counseling session being observed.

Live observation is just that—observing a session as it is happening. Live observation is the preferred method if the supervisor's goals are limited to gaining a more immediate and full view of the counselor, client, their interactions, session dynamics, and feel of the session than is possible with audiotapes and videotapes. Live observation also may provide support and reassurance for the counselor, particularly early in training ("I knew you were back there"). Worthington (1984) found that beginning supervisees gave higher ratings to supervisors who more frequently used live observation. Live observation also can be a teaching tool, as the supervisor behind the mirror can process an ongoing session with other supervisees (or supervisors-in-training).

In contrast, in *live supervision* there is the assumption that the counseling session will be interrupted at some point so that the supervisor and supervisee can interact, with the purpose of intervening in the course of the therapeutic process. As a result, there is some blurring of supervision and therapy in live supervision approaches. In fact, descriptions of some approaches emphasize the therapeutic goals over the supervisory ones. Live supervision may be the preferred approach when the supervisee could benefit from ongoing coaching during a session, or when a supervisee is working with a particularly challenging client (or group or family) or a client who is outside their developmental comfort zone.

The supervisor's particular purpose and goal also will influence the type of interruption used. *Bug-in-the-ear* (BITE) lends itself best to coaching, as the supervisor can communicate immediate suggestions ("Ask her what she has tried thus far") and reinforcements ("Good question") throughout the session. An adaptation of the BITE method is the *bug-in-the-eye* (Klitzke & Lombardo, 1991): The supervisor types comments on a keyboard that are displayed on a monitor behind the client. *Phone-in* interventions are similar to BITE interventions but occur less frequently. Typically, the supervisor is giving a directive regarding how the supervisee should proceed. These directives are brief, specific, and behavioral. They are more or less concrete, based on the developmental level of the supervisee and the complexity of the client and counseling issue (i.e., "Ask him, 'What made you decide you to come to counseling now?'" vs. "Point out the contradiction").

Consultation breaks are more geared to supervisor input or discussions regarding process issues and client conceptualization. Here, there is a well-defined break or interruption in the action, as the supervisee leaves the counseling room to consult with the supervisor. The break may come at a predetermined time during the session (e.g., at the 30-minute mark), or may be initiated by the supervisor (via a phone-in alert or a knock on the door) or by the supervisee at any point during the session (but typically during the last half). In these instances, the breaks often come when the supervisee feels stuck or the supervisor believes the session lacks direction or needs to be refocused. Consultation breaks at a predetermined time typically are more focused on identifying a final, culminating counseling intervention or homework assignment for the client. Either way, the consultation break allows time for discussion, clarification, and, hopefully, agreement on how to proceed. Lacking agreement, the supervisor must decide whether to make a directive or allow the supervisee to choose how to proceed.

There are many variations on the consultation break. These vary in their purposes, also, with many leaning more toward a therapeutic than supervisory goal. A somewhat common theme of these variations is involvement of the client or family, either as observers of the consultation or the direct receivers of the intervention. In a walk-in, the supervisor enters the counseling room and interacts with the counselor and client. Even more elaborate methods involve use of a team behind the mirror. Some methods involve the counselor going into the observation room with the team for the consultation break and discussion. Other methods involve team members agreeing to one message or intervention to be communicated to the counselor and client. The supervisor determines the tasks of team members and the procedure for determining the intervention. Anderson (1987) described a different approach that allows a client family to hear the team members' various perspectives and discussions of them. Lights and sound are turned on in the observation room or the team switches rooms with the client family and counselor. The team's discussion is as much (or more) a therapeutic intervention than feedback for the counselor.

Clearly, the purposes of team approaches are complex, and they introduce new roles and tasks for the supervisor (e.g., group organizer, group facilitator). Thus we suggest new supervisors—or those new to live supervision—begin with live observation to get accustomed to being in the observation room. Behind the one-way mirror, you can practice (in your head) determining when you might intervene, whether a phone-in or consultation break would be more appropriate, and what you would say. You might consider doing this practice with a group, so you can compare notes at the end of the session. You (and your group) also could watch a videotape of a counseling session so that you can actually stop or interrupt the session, get feedback on the appropriateness of the timing of the break, and practice the phone-in or consultation discussion (with a role-played counselor or as a team). As Bernard and Goodyear (1998) pointed out, "during-session interventions are far more complex than they may appear" (p. 137), so that measured practice sessions with a supervisor experienced with live supervision methods are greatly encouraged.

Some of the complexities of live supervision sessions lie in their timing and phrasing. Guidelines suggested by various authors (Bernard & Goodyear, 1998; Goodyear & Nelson, 1997; Liddle & Schwartz, 1983) for determining whether an intervention is needed include the following: (a) Is the interruption really needed? What likely would happen if you did not interrupt?; (b) Is the supervisee likely to come up with the desired intervention during the session?; (c) Can the counselor actually carry out the desired intervention?; (d) How will the intervention affect the momentum of the session at this particular moment?; (e) Can the consultation break be conducted in an appropriate amount of time, or does the discussion need to be held for a regular supervision review session?; (f) Will your directive encourage counselor dependency on the supervisor?; and (g) Is your directive based on client needs, supervisee needs, or your wish to be the counselor? Obviously, the latter motivation is an inappropriate goal or purpose of live supervision!

There also are guidelines for delivering phone-in messages (Bernard & Goodyear, 1998; Goodyear & Nelson, 1997; Wright, 1986), including the following: (a) Make the statements brief, specific, and action-oriented; (b) avoid process statements; (c) be conservative, aiming for three to five directives per counseling session; (d) give no more than two instructions per phone-in; (e) avoid making phone-ins during the first 10 minutes of a session; (f) begin with a positive statement about what has happened thus far; (g) make the wording appropriate to the counselor's developmental level (e.g., "Ask her ...vs. "Explore..."); (h) model the wording and the attitude you want the counselor to convey to the client; and (i) make sure the counselor understands your message and call for a consultation break if needed.

Several procedural points need to be addressed before implementing a live supervision method. In fact, Bubenzer, Mahrle, and West (1987) suggested supervisees benefit from practice via role-plays first. Preliminary discussions also should include explicit attention to the roles and rules for the participation of all involved (Bernard & Goodyear, 1998; Elizur, 1990; Montalvo, 1973), such as who can call for a consultation break and for what reasons, whether the supervisee is required to carry out any supervisor directive or what flexibility the supervisee has to use the directive, and basic agreement about using a particular live supervision method. The client also needs to be fully informed and give consent to the purposes and procedures of the method to be used, including expectations of the client (e.g., types of interactions with the supervisor or team members).

It should be noted that a live supervision session takes place within the context of a presession planning discussion and a postsession debriefing (Bernard & Goodyear, 1998). In the preliminary meeting, the purpose and goals of the observation are clarified. Ideally, these are framed within some of the supervisee's own learning goals. Any other preparation for the session also is conducted. Depending on the supervisee's developmental level, this may include role-playing a technique to be used or creating a general outline for the upcoming session. If a team approach is to be used, the team also may be involved in the pre-session so that members' roles and participation responsibilities are made clear. In the postsession debriefing, feedback and discussion again is framed around the purposes and goals of the live supervision. Now is the time for discussion of process issues and client conceptualization. Some follow-up discussion a few days later also may be needed, as the supervisee likely will achieve further insights and questions that become clear only with some distance from the live supervision event.

The advantages and disadvantages of live supervision methods have been debated widely (see Bernard & Goodyear, 1998, for an informative summary), and the lack of research evidence for either also has been noted (Bernard & Goodyear, 1998; Goodyear & Nelson, 1997). Perhaps importantly, few of the disadvantages have been supported. Of course, it should be remembered that there is very limited research on the efficacy of any supervision method.

Cognitive Counseling Skills

Most of the supervision interventions presented thus far have been focused on developing counseling performance skills and counselor self-awareness. Much less attention has been given to the development of cognitive counseling skills in the literature, perhaps because these skills are difficult to isolate and describe due to their covert nature. "How do we get inside counselors' heads" is a challenging question for supervisors and researchers. Nevertheless, "it is striking how much of the supervision literature points to supervisees' cognitions as the underlying, if not primary, focus of supervisory work" (Borders, 2001, p. 425). This is true in the theoretical, empirical, and practice-oriented supervision literature.

Developmental models of supervision are based in theories of cognitive development, including those of Piaget (Piaget & Inhelder, 1969), Loevinger (1976), and Harvey, Hunt, and Schroeder (1961). As stated in chapter 1 (this volume), the cognitive basis for these models is perhaps best described by Blocher (1983), who emphasized that the supervisor's task is to encourage supervisee movement toward a very high level of functioning. Others have drawn from the expert-novice literature (Martin, Slemon, Hiebert, Hallberg, & Cummings, 1989; Skovholt & Jennings, 2004; Skovholt & Rønnestad, 1992a, 1992b; Skovholt, Rønnestad, & Jennings, 1997), which emphasizes differences in conceptual processes of beginners and experts in various professions. In fact, the development and description of counselor expertise was the focus of several comprehensive qualitative studies by Skovholt and colleagues (Skovholt & Jennings, 2004; Skovholt & Rønnestad, 1992a, 1992b). Although their analyses yielded topics other than conceptual theme categories (e.g., influences of personal life, clients, and mentors; emotional wellness and ethical values), cognitions were a central underlying component.

There are several common themes across the developmental models and the expert-novice writings. Experts (not to be confused with more experienced counselors) have more knowledge and can handle much larger amounts of information more effectively and efficiently, primarily because of their enhanced ability to "chunk" information into large, more meaningful patterns and principles (vs. the novice's focus on isolated details and theoretical rules). Experts seem to spend a good deal of time up-front analyzing a problem, differentiating between what information is really important and which is actually needed to solve the problem. Importantly, high-functioning professionals seek out, value, and can handle multiple perspectives, including various theoretical perspectives as well as diverse cultural frameworks. They embrace inconsistencies, ambiguities, paradoxes, and ill-structured problems that do not have one right solution. Their solutions, based in accumulated wisdom (Skovholt & Rønnestad, 1992a, 1992b) developed over many years, are creative, if not idiosyncratic, and tailored to a particular situation or client.

So, the desired outcomes in cognitive counseling skills training are richly described—at least in broad terms—and have a fairly strong empirical basis. How do we help novice counselors move toward high levels of cognitive functioning and expertise? Blocher (1983) and Skovholt and Rønnestad (1992a) both emphasized learning environments that provide a balance of challenge and support, opportunities for innovation and integration, but offered few specifics.

Skovholt and Rønnestad (1992a) found that continuous professional reflection was a central process for moving from novice to expert. This process is similar to descriptions of the reflective process (e.g., Neufeldt, Karno, & Nelson, 1996), based on Schön's (1983) ideas regarding educating reflective practitioners. Similar to the principles described above, reflective learning requires a meaningful problem at an appropriate level of challenge and ambiguity, and a safe environment to explore the problem, as well as how one's personal and professional experiences inform and influence their process.

In the practice-oriented literature on cognitive skills, formats or models of case conceptualization, sometimes also referred to as clinical hypothesis formation, are most frequently mentioned (Borders, 2001). (See Borders & Leddick, 1987, and Nelson & Neufeldt, 1998, for an overview of several formats.) Case conceptualization formats certainly are useful in helping counselors be systematic and thorough and learn the variety of information relevant to clinical decision making, particularly when they are applied to supervisees' actual clients. Some variation of a case conceptualization framework often is used as the basis for case presentations in group supervision. Given the static quality of these formats, however, deliberate supervisory methods are needed if case conceptualization applications are to incorporate the principles of reflective practice, expertise, and high levels of cognitive functioning. Neufeldt et al. (1995) provided examples of supervision strategies that encourage case conceptualization and reflection of trainees in their first practicum experience (see chap. 4, this volume, for some relevant suggestions for group supervision).

Similarly, process notes encourage introspection and reflective thinking (see description, earlier in this chapter). Even standard case notes can be used toward this end, with appropriate discussion and application. Presser and Pfost (1985), for example, found that beginning supervisees tended to have an almost exclusive focus on the client in their case notes. With experience and training, however, they began to include observations and inferences about their own in-session behavior, and then reciprocal influence and interactional patterns in the counseling relationship.

Although these methods are useful within the larger picture, they do not get to the in-session level of cognitive processing—the place where moment-by-moment observations are analyzed, evaluated, and translated into a counselor response or intervention. One way to assess and teach such skills is the *thinking-aloud* approach. For example, a typical sequence might go like this: The supervisor notes that the supervisee seems to be unaware of or ignoring the client's tearfulness. The supervisor asks, "What do you remember noticing about your client's reaction here?" The counselor reports that she was surprised by her client's verbal response, and didn't know what to say. The supervisor then says:

> As I'm watching your client here on the videotape, I'm confused, too. For several sessions she has been talking about how there is really nothing left in her marriage, and the positive qualities of the other man she is seeing. Yet, when you ask her what's missing in her marriage, she replies, "Hope; hope that it will get better." And I see her reach for a tissue and it looks like she tears up. So, at this moment in the session I'm wondering how to make sense of all this. It almost seems like she hasn't given up on her marriage. I get some sense that she's searching for something, something deep and really meaningful. I sense such grief in her body, the way she is slumped over, her tears, her reference to hope. And I'm wondering how I could check that out, how I could help her get to that level.

In essence, the supervisor has modeled a thinking process meant to work on multiple levels. The supervisor's thinking-aloud statements include (a) observations of a client's words and nonverbal behavior (reminding the supervisee to watch both!); (b) the value of comparing today's client behavior with behaviors in previous sessions; (c) an acceptance of contradictions in a client's behavior, which are viewed as meaningful rather than wrong; (d) an awareness of internal responses to a client and what helpful insights they may offer; (e) one way to put together all this information; and (f) an openness to checking out a hypothesis about the client's pain versus having to figure it out before saying or doing anything. Through this thinking-aloud sequence, the supervisor has given the counselor some new perspectives on (and hopefully greater empathy for) her client, and taken the supervisory conversation about the client to a new level. Importantly, the tone is nonjudgmental—not "why didn't you see this and think this." In fact, the supervisor states up front that these are her observations and thoughts as she watches the client on the videotape versus the demanding position of being in-session with a client. Nevertheless, the supervisee has been introduced to some other ways of thinking about her client during a session which, over time and with more supervision and practice, hopefully she also may achieve.

When thinking aloud, the supervisor wants to achieve the developmentally appropriate half-step challenge and avoid overwhelming the supervisee. Of course, a supervisor's thinking aloud can be at quite sophisticated levels, about transference and countertransference, reciprocal interpersonal dynamics, and other latent issues. As implied thus far, the supervisor's spoken-aloud thoughts may be carefully crafted to help the supervisee move forward. At other times, they may be actual spontaneous thoughts (i.e., the supervisor truly is confused), offered to the more advanced supervisee for mutual discussion and exploration. It should be noted that the expert, cognitively complex counselor/

supervisor may model an idiosyncratic pattern of analysis and problem solving (Blocher, 1983; Skovholt & Rønnestad, 1992a, 1992b), which may need to be clarified for advanced supervisees, who are then encouraged to develop their own individualized processes, grounded in their own professional experiences.

When the goal is to assess or identify the supervisee's in-session cognitions, the thinking-aloud approach begins to have an IPR flavor. IPR supervisor leads that encourage recall of in-session thoughts include questions such as "What thoughts were you having about the other person at that time?," "Did you have any plan of where you wanted the session to go next?," and "Did you think the other person knew what you wanted?" (see Bernard & Goodyear, 1998, p. 102).

Another way to tap into unexpressed, even unconscious, thoughts and feelings about a client is through the use of metaphors. Metaphors also may enhance case conceptualization skills (Young & Borders, 1998, 1999). As needed, supervisors can suggest a general metaphor to be applied and explored for a particular client (or group or couple or family) or counseling relationship (e.g., the "dance" during a session), or ask supervisees to identify or create their own metaphors. Similarly, Ishiyama (1988) and Amundson (1988) have described the use of visual metaphors (drawings) in supervision. Increasingly, we also are seeing the use of the symbolic methods of play therapy used in supervision, although there are as yet few descriptions in the literature (see Dean, 2001, for one example). A key to the usefulness of any metaphor is how it is processed—what insights it provides about the client and clinical issue, the counselor's experience of or reaction to the client, and so forth, as well as what happens next ("playing out the metaphor"). Thus, a supervisor's skill with processing is critical to the effectiveness of these interventions.

Summary

We have described a representative sample of interventions a supervisor may use in individual supervision sessions. Our emphasis has been on raising awareness of the issues that can affect a supervisor's choices, as well as factors that should be considered in making deliberate, proactive choices that encourage supervisee development. Skill in preparing for a session is as important as implementing a plan during a session. The art of conducting supervision is becoming clearer.

Discussion Questions

1. At the end of Chapter 1, you were asked to indicate what supervisor roles and focus areas you most likely would use. Now, complete the Supervisor Emphasis Rating Form—Revised (SERF-R; Lanning, 1986; Lanning & Freeman, 1994) and the Supervisory Styles Inventory (SSI; Friedlander & Ward, 1984), included in this chapter, using the scoring rubrics for each below.

Scoring Key for the SERF-R

Supervisor Emphasis Rating Form—Revised

	Professional Behaviors	*Counseling Performance Skills*	*Self-Awareness*	*Cognitive Counseling Skills*
Set 1	A	B	C	D
Set 2	A	D	C	B
Set 3	D	B	C	A
Set 4	D	C	B	A
Set 5	C	B	A	D
Set 6	B	C	A	D
Set 7	D	C	B	A
Set 8	B	D	C	A
Set 9	B	A	C	D
Set 10	B	D	C	A
Set 11	C	B	A	D
Set 12	B	A	D	C
Set 13	A	D	C	B
Set 14	D	A	C	B
Set 15	B	C	A	D

Attractive
Sum your ratings on items 15, 16, 22, 23, 29, 30, 33, and divide by 7 for the mean score.
Interpersonally sensitive
Sum your ratings on items 2, 5, 10, 11, 21, 25, 26, 28, and divide by 8 for the mean score.
Task-oriented
Sum your ratings on items 1, 3, 4, 7, 13, 14, 17, 18, 19, 20, and divide by 10 for the mean score.

In what ways were your results on these assessments similar to and different from your earlier responses? Were there any surprises? Do you have any additional goals based on your results?

2. What contextual factors need to be considered in your current or upcoming supervision work? To what extent does your context affect your choice of supervision interventions?
3. Which supervision interventions have you experienced as a supervisee? How was each helpful and not helpful? Which seem most appropriate for your current supervisee, in your current supervisory context?
4. Which supervision interventions have you used? How would you rate the success of those interventions? What might have influenced your degree of success with them? Describe your rationale for choosing a particular intervention for a particular supervision session.
5. IPR is based in phenomenological theories. Could a cognitive-behavioral-oriented supervisor find this approach useful?

6. Practice IPR and live supervision as suggested in this chapter (i.e., using a videotaped session, observing while constructing your live supervision intervention in your head, etc.). Do the same with the thinking-aloud approach.
7. You are supervising Lin, an Asian-American female in her late twenties. She is completing her school counseling practicum, has 3 years of middle-school teaching experience, and appears to be intelligent and very outspoken. As a student, Lin is struggling financially, which places her under much internal stress. She presented herself as quite sure of her individual counseling skills, until you provided feedback on her first counseling tape. In this first counseling session, Lin functioned as a problem solver, trying to "fix it" in one session, without even really engaging the client in the process. She bombarded the client with question after question, then ended the session by saying, "Here's what I think you should do…" and sending the client out with the assignment. When confronted with this in the supervision session, Lin argued politely with you, still seemingly convinced that she had done the right thing, yet appearing quite anxious about the feedback.

    a. What is your greatest concern with Lin's current behavior in supervision?
    b. What intervention would you use with Lin next?
    c. Explain your rationale for the selected intervention.

Chapter 4

Group Supervision

Regardless of your setting, it is highly likely that you will provide group as well as individual supervision for your supervisees. Both accreditation standards (CACREP, 2001) and counselor licensure regulations (Borders & Cashwell, 1992; Sutton, 1997) require the experience of group supervision as well as individual supervision. Why? It is believed that the group experience provides supervisees with an important and unique learning context. Groups can provide a supportive environment of peers who likely have similar concerns and questions, comparable skills and goals.

In groups, supervisees have the opportunity to learn from each other through feedback, brainstorming, and exposure to a wider variety of clients and clinical issues. In fact, novice counselors communicate with each other quite effectively in groups—perhaps better than the supervisor communicates with them—as they speak the same language and model achievable skills (Hillerbrand, 1989). They may recognize each other's anxiety cues or confusion more quickly than their supervisor does. As a result, group members can be powerful motivators for each other, thereby encouraging risk taking and increasing self-efficacy. Similar dynamics may be found in groups of more experienced counselors, who seek consultation and feedback about difficult clients from their peers. Coming together also may help them deal with burnout and isolation (Lewis, Greenburg, & Hatch, 1988), as well as frustrations with their setting (i.e., managed-care restrictions, school principal's requirements).

Supervision groups may provide these many opportunities for learning, personal growth, and professional collaboration. And they may not, depending on how they are conducted. Several considerations are key to a group's success. First, supervision groups are groups, and thus are subject to the dynamics present in all groups, including dynamics that can both facilitate and impede positive outcomes. Needed is a group leader or facilitator who attends to group process, deals with competitive or protective dynamics, and sees today's group as part of the larger supervision context. In short, supervision groups need a skilled supervisor with strong group leadership and group facilitation skills.

DOI: 10.4324/9781003251583-4

In addition, supervision groups need structure, purpose, and direction, given that they are more task oriented than counseling groups (Kruger, Cherniss, Maher, & Leichtman, 1988; Werstlein & Borders, 1997). The group supervisor, then, needs to carefully consider why this group is meeting, why these particular counselors are in this group, and what success would mean for this group—as differentiated from individual supervision with these same counselors. In other words, what do you want to happen in this group that is different from what happens (or can't happen) in individual supervision? This doesn't mean that the supervisor unilaterally makes all the decisions for a supervision group. Coconstruction of goals, agreement regarding member responsibilities, and even endorsement of a group procedure or format facilitate members' ownership of the group and their accountability to each other. Nevertheless, the supervisor carries major responsibilities for helping the group be effective and productive, including providing an appropriate structure as well as pointing out the dynamics that are impeding the work of the group.

A group leader's decisions about a supervision group will be influenced by a number of relevant factors, including the experience and developmental levels of the counselors, members' work settings (e.g., schools, community agencies, private practice), and the purpose and goals that brought this group together. Sometimes, group supervisors have previous knowledge of members' personality dynamics that also may influence their group plans (e.g., competitiveness, avoidance, dependency, openness, difficulty dealing with persons in authority). In addition, practical factors need to be considered: How often will this group meet? Where? Over how many weeks? How many counselors will be in the group? These factors—plus those specific to any particular group—will guide the supervisor's planning for group supervision.

As with counseling groups, the first group supervision session is a key one for setting the tone and expectations for this experience. Supervisors need to give deliberate thought to their goals and priorities for the group, as well as how these can be communicated—and put into action—during the first group session. Most supervisors, for example, want all group members to participate actively in each group. How can you help that happen in the first session? Possibilities range from structured ice-breaker activities to open-ended discussion questions (e.g., "Here are my hopes for this group and how we will interact with each other…; How can we make that happen? What can you contribute to making this happen in this group?").

Also consider how well group members already know each other, and how much they need to know about each other to function as the group you environment. The first group session certainly can be a time for group members to share learning goals. It also may be a time for member to state what they hope to gain from the group, why they decided to join this group, what kinds of group experiences (positive and not so positive) they have had in the past, or how they see themselves as multicultural beings. These are merely suggestions for the first supervision group, meant to illustrate the kind of issues supervisors need to consider in planning for the group. You will want to make your own plan based on the purpose of the group, your priorities for the group atmosphere and functioning, the needs of the group members, and other relevant factors. Importantly, you also will be sending a message about your role to members during the first group, whether you talk about your role directly or not. In fact, as always, what you do in your role will be more powerful than what you say about your role.

Group Supervisor's Role

In line with our previous discussions of a supervisor's role, the group supervisor's foremost responsibility is to facilitate group members' learning. Often, the learning process in a group revolves around a case presentation by a group member. Typically, the designated presenter provides background information about a particular client (oral or written), identifies questions and specific requests for feedback, responds to initial questions of group members, presents an audiotaped or videotaped segment of a session illustrating the supervision issue, receives feedback from group members, and summarizes the feedback, including comments on its usefulness and, perhaps, reactions to the feedback. You probably noticed that the supervisor is not mentioned in this agenda or group procedure. So, what is the supervisor's role in such a group session?

First, the supervisor likely chose the format for group case presentations. The supervisor will have determined the amount of direction and structure needed by a particular supervision group and may have provided an outline or training for the identified approach. For more experienced groups, the supervisor may have chosen to let the group members determine their own procedure. The supervisor, of course, may offer feedback or observations about the group members' decisions (e.g., to what extent the procedure fits with group goals, allows for honest feedback, involves all group members, etc.), including whether the supervisor believes she can work successfully with the group using this procedure. Regardless, once the procedure is determined, the supervisor's goal is to have the group (eventually) essentially run itself following the procedure.

The supervisor's role, then, becomes more of a learning facilitator and commentator on in-the-moment dynamics that seem to be affecting the learning process. The supervisor poses a question to a quiet member that draws on her strengths, comments on the sense that something important is not being addressed in the group discussion, identifies group members' feelings of helplessness that mirror the client's and counselor's feelings of helplessness, observes the impact of a member's willingness to risk. In short, the group supervisor uses the group itself as a tool for learning, intervening, prodding. In fact, the negative effects of a supervisor's lack of attention to group process has been documented (Linton, 2003). As a commentator on group process, the supervisor facilitates learning about clinical dynamics, encourages self-awareness and personal growth, and serves as a role model of a group leader and skilled counselor.

The supervisor also is an observer and commentator about the content of the group discussion. Here, the supervisor facilitates learning via comments or questions that help group members make connections, identify underlying principles and themes, or question their assumptions. These interventions illustrate the supervisor's responsibility to help the group be a learning experience for all group members, not just the counselor who has made the case presentation of the day. In essence, each group session typically provides one to three lessons that the supervisor searches for and helps group members recognize. The discussion then becomes somewhat more general, or generalized, as each group member is encouraged to consider how today's lessons could be applied in their own work. Each group member, then, should leave with a new idea, perspective, or insight that they can try out with an upcoming client, and may even bring back a report for further discussion during the next group meeting. Often, these learnings or lessons are not totally new; they may involve concepts, dynamics, or skills covered in previous courses. Their application with various clients, however, helps bring out their nuances or necessary variations in tailoring them for specific clients, thus deepening the counselors' understanding of the concepts, dynamics, and skills.

Thus, the group supervisor's role involves attention to both process and content. In fact, the group supervisor's task is to find the needed, appropriate balance of focus on content versus process within a group session, and across group sessions, for a particular group. This balance in focus exists within the larger task of balancing challenge and support in supervision. Here, the artistry of a group supervisor's work is clear.

Structured Peer Group Model

The dual focus on content and process is evident in published models of group supervision (e.g., Borders, 1991; Christensen & Kline, 2001; Wilbur, Roberts-Wilbur, Morris, Betz, & Hart, 1991). For purposes of illustration, we describe and discuss Borders' (1991) structured peer group format, as we have employed this approach in a variety of settings, including academic and field settings, with counselors-in-training and experienced counselors, and we have been involved in research about the model (e.g., Crutchfield & Borders, 1997). Like other published models, the structured peer group format illustrates the group supervisor's purposeful, deliberate educational planning that effective group supervisors give to their work (Borders, 2001).

Similar to other group supervision models, Borders' (1991) model is based in a case presentation approach (see Table 4.1 for an overview outline). During initial meetings, group members identify and share learning goals. In addition, group procedures, rules, and expectations are clarified. Explanation of

Table 4.1 Structured Peer Group Supervision

1. The **counselor** identifies questions about the client or videotaped session, and requests specific feedback.
   What I need help with ...
   What I'm unsure of ...
   Help me rephrase this more effectively.
   Help me understand my feelings of frustration toward this client.
   Help me be less hesitant when confronting, as I am in this session.
   I want to be less of an advice-giver.
   How did I get into this yes/but routine with this client?
   Am I laying my values on this client?
2. **Peers** (other counselors) choose or are assigned roles, perspectives, or tasks for reviewing the videotape segment:
   Focused observations of
   counselor nonverbal behavior
   client nonverbal behavior
   particular counseling skill
   Role-taking
   client
   counselor
   parent, spouse, coworker, friend, teacher, or other significant person in the client's life
   Theoretical perspectives on the
   Assessment of client
   Conceptualization of the issue or problem
   Goals of counseling
   Choice of interventions (*how* to choose and *what* to choose)
   Evaluation of progress
   Descriptive metaphors for
   client
   counselor
   counseling process
3. The counselor presents the videotape segment.
4. Peers give feedback from their roles or perspective, keeping in mind the goals and questions that were specified by the counselor.
5. The **supervisor** facilitates the discussion as needed, functioning in two roles:
   Moderator who helps the group stay on-task by
   a) Helping the presenting counselor articulate a specific focus for the supervision session.
   b) Assigning and/or designating roles and tasks for the group members.
   c) Making sure everyone is heard and is following feedback guidelines.
   d) Summarizing the feedback, identifying themes and patterns (e.g., each time the client teared the counselor asked a question).
   e) Setting up follow-up exercises as needed (e.g., role-plays or directed skill practice).
   Process commentator who serves as a group leader by
   a) Giving feedback on the dynamics of the peer group.
   b) Encouraging discussion of behaviors, feelings, and relationships.

(*Continued*)

Table 4.1 (Continued)

c) Being sensitive to members' reactions to feedback, including ways they may protect or compete with each other.
d) Being aware of manifestations of parallel process.

6. The supervisor summarizes the feedback and discussion, and the counselor indicates if supervision needs were met.

Based on Borders, L. D. (1991). A systematic approach to peer group supervision. *Journal of Counseling and Development, 69*, 248–252.

the structured peer group model also is provided. In subsequent sessions, the designated counselor for the day presents oral or written background information on a client, and then requests specific feedback. Group members then choose or are assigned roles, perspectives, or tasks they will use to guide their review of a videotaped or audiotaped segment of a recent counseling session with the client (or group, or family, etc.). These tasks may include (a) *focused observations* of counselor or client nonverbal behavior, a particular counseling skill, or a particular session event (e.g., termination); (b) *role-taking*, or viewing the taped session segment from the perspective of the client, counselor, or relevant persons in the client's life, such as the client's parent, teacher, spouse, co-worker, or friend (or another member of the counseling group or a family member present in the family counseling session); (c) *theoretical perspectives*, which involves viewing the session segment from a particular theoretical perspective as related to client assessment, explanation of the client's issue or presenting problem, appropriate counseling goals for this client, appropriate interventions for working with this client, and evaluation of the client's progress (or the same for a counseling group or family); and (d) *descriptive metaphors* for the client, counselor, counseling interaction or process, client family system, the counseling group, and so forth. The counselor then presents the taped segment of the counseling session. Following this, the group members give feedback from their roles or perspectives. At the end of this exchange and discussion, the supervisor or presenting counselor summarizes the feedback and, perhaps, how it will be applied in the next counseling session. Finally, the counselor indicates the extent to which supervision needs have been met.

Within these steps, the group supervisor takes on process and content roles and determines the amount of directiveness and structure needed for a particular counselor or group session. In the role of *moderator*, the supervisor attends to session content and lessons that can be drawn from the content. There also is a managerial component to the moderator role, as the supervisor helps the group stay on task, oversees role assignments, makes sure feedback guidelines are followed, and everyone has a turn. In the moderator role, the supervisor can vary the directiveness of any task, based on an assessment of structure needed at any particular time. For example, in early sessions, the supervisor may assign roles, and do so deliberately, based on knowledge of the group members (e.g., assigning a group member a goal relevant to his or her own learning goals, such as better observation of client nonverbal behavior or gaining greater depth in understanding and applying a particular counseling theory). Later, the supervisor may decide group members are ready to be introduced to larger, more process-oriented and abstract concepts, and so ask all group members to think metaphorically, even providing a common and "easy" metaphor (e.g., dance) for all to use the first time this perspective is attempted. As the group becomes more comfortable with the structured peer group approach, and as group members begin to take more responsibility for the group, the presenting counselor may want to assign roles, or group members may want to volunteer for roles and perspectives. The group supervisor then takes on more of a monitoring role (e.g., does one group member volunteer for the same role each week?) and can give more energy and attention to process rather than content.

As a *process commentator*, the group supervisor shares observations about group dynamics, including ways that group members seem to compete with or protect each other. The supervisor makes comments designed to encourage more depth in the exploration of roles and perspectives (e.g., to the client role, "Would you repeat that feedback in first person, I, speaking as the client?" "When you turned your head away at that point, what were you thinking?," "What did you want the counselor to say or do?," and "What did you want to say but didn't say to your counselor?").

What is difficult to describe in this (and any other) model are the subtleties of the group supervisor's role. We have seen this approach bomb when the supervisor was overly directive, failed to address destructive group dynamics, or allowed the discussion to remain at a theoretical or superficial level. We have also observed great "ah-hah" moments, counselor self-confrontation, and honest and caring sharing. No model can do the job of group supervision. A supervisor's skill, artistry, and sensitivity are necessary conditions for any approach to be effective—to be as powerful as it is capable of being. Thus, we encourage new group supervisors, or supervisor trying out a new group approach, to seek feedback from colleagues and group members, and self-supervise via videotapes of your group supervision sessions. Sometimes, the focus on learning and using a new procedure can crowd out what we know about counseling, groups, and learning. Your clinical and educational experience, however, should be at the forefront, as these are the skills that bring creativity, sensitivity, and elegance to a group supervisor's work.

Importantly, the design of the structured peer group approach grew out of specified goals for a particular group supervision experience. The structured peer group approach originally was designed to address seven goals (Borders,

1991): (a) to have all group members participate in the supervision process; (b) to help members give feedback that is focused and objective; (c) to emphasize development of cognitive counseling skills; (d) to create an approach that can be adapted to meet the needs of both novice and experienced counselors; (e) to create an approach applicable to supervision of individual, group, and family counseling sessions; (f) to teach self-monitoring skills; and (g) to provide a model structured and straightforward enough for novice supervisors to use, yet flexible enough—and capable of allowing for depth and complexity of supervision work—for use by experienced supervisors whose goals are similar to those highlighted by the model. To these goals can be added the intention of creating an approach that (h) encourages self-growth of group members and (i) facilitates members' awareness of counseling process and group dynamics. These may or may not be goals relevant to your group.

As we have consistently stated, it is necessary to first determine what you want to accomplish in any supervision enterprise. The methods, procedures, and activities chosen for a supervision experience, including group supervision, should be firmly rooted in the designated learning goals. The supervisor's goals for the group do not ignore counselors' learning goals. Rather, the supervisor's goals typically subsume individual supervisee's goals because they are larger and broader. Thus, we encourage you to adapt the structured peer group model—or any model—in ways that make it more appropriate for your work with a particular group.

Discussion Questions

1. Consider a supervision group you have led, are about to lead, or would like to lead or facilitate. How would you describe your role to group members during the first group supervision session? What changes in the group would lead you to change your view of your role?
2. Describe your goals for your current or upcoming supervision group. What degree of structure is needed? What methods or format would be an appropriate match for this group?
3. What are your strengths as a group leader and group counselor? How do or will you use these in group supervision?
4. While meeting with your supervision group for the third time, you become aware that David, a Latin American male intern, is having difficulty giving appropriate feedback to his peers in the group. He is quick to point out everything the other supervisees did wrong with their clients, and just as quick to tell them what he would have done. Although some of his "suggestions" have merit, he seems to prefer a directive, problem-solving approach with his clients, just as he prefers to be directive when giving feedback to other group members. As he continues to do this, two of the other supervisees appear to shut down, saying very little in response to

his feedback to them. In your view, David seems to be monopolizing the group, more so in this session than in the last one.

a. How would you address the process of group dynamics within this third group session?
b. Describe your rationale for this approach.
c. What are the possible cultural implications?

Chapter 5

Supervisory Relationship and Process Issues

The supervisory relationship is the heart and soul of the supervision experience, regardless of the experience and developmental level of the supervisee (Rønnestad & Skovholt, 1993). In fact, many believe a supervisor's ability to create and maintain a positive working relationship with supervisees is as important—or more important—than technical supervisory skills (Borders, 1994; Dye, 1994). A safe, trusting environment, characterized by mutual respect, is required for a supervisee to be open to feedback, to be willing to learn and change (Borders, 2001).

Creating such an environment is a tall order, particularly given the evaluative nature of supervision. Supervisees are asked to be vulnerable and self-disclose their professional inadequacies and their personal biases to the same person who will grade them, write letters of recommendation, or complete reference forms for licensure. Some supervisors try to downplay their power and evaluative responsibilities. This is a detriment to the supervisory relationship because it is not honest; both the supervisor and the supervisee know that, at some point, the evaluation must and will come (see also chap. 7, this volume). The exception may be supervisees at the highest developmental levels who seek periodic consultation from a colleague-supervisor. Most of your supervision work, however, most likely will be with supervisees in training programs and internship, in prelicensure positions, or in agencies that require periodic employee evaluations. The evaluative aspect of supervision does not need to be a focus or emphasis each week, but we should beware of pretending that it does not exist.

Although the supervisory relationship is pivotal to the learning process, it is difficult to describe and nearly impossible to prescribe. The steps of a supervision intervention can be set out in an almost formulaic manner, but success and effectiveness of any intervention delivery is highly dependent on the supervisor's skill in interacting with the supervisee before, during, and after the intervention. In other words, the dynamics of a particular supervisor-supervisee relationship are unique and even idiosyncratic. Yes, trust is a necessary factor, but supervisees differ in their willingness to trust. Yes, gender is always at play in supervision, but no two female or male supervisees are

DOI: 10.4324/9781003251583-5

exactly alike in terms of how their gender influences their behaviors, beliefs, expectations, and motivations (Hoffman, Borders, & Hattie, 2000). Yes, race and ethnicity necessarily influence the supervisory relationship, whether or not acknowledged, but neither person in the dyad is defined by their race and ethnicity alone nor do they necessarily share the same experiences and attitudes even if they share the same racial and ethnic background (see also Leong & Wagner, 1994). Other illustrations could be provided, but the point probably is clear. Each supervisee—and supervisor—brings unique personalities, life experiences, interpersonal histories, professional motivations and goals to the supervisory context. Each supervisory relationship, then, is unique, and what works with one supervisee will not work in exactly the same way with another supervisee—or even that same supervisee at a different point in time. This is the art of supervision.

Fortunately, counseling supervisors are well-trained in theories and skills relevant to creating a productive, effective supervisory relationship. As discussed in chapter 1 (this volume), the supervisor's counseling background is highly relevant to understanding the person of the supervisee and how that person behaves as a professional—in counseling and supervision sessions.

Components of the Supervisory Relationship

In an effort to delineate the critical components of the supervisory relationship, several theories have been applied to supervisor-supervisee interactions. Theories from the fields of counseling, education, social psychology, and communication have been explored conceptually and empirically. (We offer these as examples not an inclusive list.) Not surprisingly, Rogerian core conditions for facilitating a relationship have been of interest (e.g., Pierce & Schauble, 1970, 1971; Schact, Howe, & Berman, 1988). Similarly, Bordin (1983) extended his working alliance model of therapeutic change to the supervision context. Efstation, Patton, and Kardash (1990) developed the Supervisory Working Alliance Inventory based on Bordin's model. This is one of the few measures created from study of the supervision enterprise (vs. adapting a counseling-based measure by changing *counselor* to *supervisor*). More recently, the relevance of Bowlby's (1973) attachment theory for supervision relationships has been explored (e.g., Neswald-McCalip, 2001; Pistole & Watkins, 1995; Watkins, 1995; White & Queener, 2003). From the teacher education literature, Blumberg's (1968) Interactional Analysis model has been used to identify verbal behaviors and interactional patterns of supervisor and supervisees (e.g., Holloway & Wampold, 1983).

From social psychology, supervision researchers have found relevance in Strong's (1968) social influence theory (e.g., Claiborn, Etringer, & Hillerbrand, 1995; Dixon & Claiborn, 1987); self-presentation, role conflict, and role ambiguity (Friedlander et al., 1986; Ladany & Friedlander, 1995; Ward, Friedlander, Schoen, & Klein, 1985); and the elaboration likelihood model

(Claiborn et al., 1995; Petty & Cacioppo, 1986; Stoltenberg, McNeill, & Crethar, 1995). In addition, Holloway's (1995, 1997) systems approach to supervision (SAS) draws on Penman's (1980) communication matrix, which in turn is based in Leary's (1957) circumplex model. In particular, Holloway has explored the dynamics of power and involvement as central to the supervision relationship.

All of these applications, or extrapolations, are instructive, and each has its limitations in covering the full gamut involved in the supervision relationship. It may be that supervisors draw on the related theories and constructs, such as those cited previously, with which they already are familiar (cf. Bradley & Gould, 2001; Friedlander & Ward, 1984). Perhaps our preferred frameworks, which have worked well for us in the past, serve as a useful background for understanding the interpersonal and relational aspects of new experiences, such as supervision. If so, this can be both helpful and limiting, because any theory and framework has its advantages and disadvantages, which we would need to acknowledge and address. Thus, articulating your own relevant theories and preferences could be a useful exercise, so that they could be examined and assessed during your supervisory relationships.

Multicultural Influences on the Supervisory Relationship

Other supervision researchers have focused on demographic-type variables such as gender, race, ethnicity, and sexual orientation. Given the society in which we live, it is no surprise that these social variables influence supervisor-supervisee interactions, although, as Nelson and Holloway (1990) wrote, "they are subtle and highly complex" (p. 478). Thus, these influences also are difficult to recognize—and modify—in our supervisees' behaviors, as well as our own. Even so, these variables may be too static and oversimplified. For example, gender, racial, and gay or lesbian *identity* may be more salient (Borders, 2001; Ellis & Ladany, 1997; Hays & Chang, 2003). Nevertheless, there is consistent evidence that typical power dynamics related to gender influence supervision interactions. Both male and female supervisors seem to behave in ways that grant more power to their male than female supervisees, such as asking males their opinions more often (Nelson & Holloway, 1999). There also are some indications that male-male dyads may focus more on the client while female-female dyads are more relational oriented (Sells, Goodyear, Lichtenberg, & Polkinghorne, 1997), and female supervisees may underestimate their skills while male supervisees overestimate their effectiveness (Warburton, Newberry, & Alexander, 1989). Power also is a central theme in multicultural supervision (Cook, 1994; Fong & Lease, 1997; Hays & Chang, 2003). In the typical White-supervisor/supervisee-of-color dyad, the supervisor has dual power as a majority person in an evaluative position. Similar dynamics have been noted for sexual minority supervisees (Burhke, 1988, 1989).

There is some evidence that supervisors believe they make more efforts to address multicultural issues than their supervisees perceive (Duan & Roehlke, 2001), but discussion of cultural variables does have positive outcomes enhancing the supervisory relationship as well as supervisees' overall satisfaction (Gatmon et al., 2001). Importantly, Gatmon et al. (2001) included discussion not only of differences and similarities on race and ethnicity, but also gender and sexual orientation. As emphasized in chapter 2 (this volume), it is the supervisor's responsibility to introduce multicultural issues early in the supervision relationship, check in about them often, and invite the supervisee to discuss them at any time, regarding both the counseling and the supervision relationships. In addition, as suggested in the descriptions of developmental models (see chap. 1, this volume, and Leong & Wagner, 1994), supervisees will differ in their ability to recognize, discuss, and act on multicultural issues.

Given the broader social context within which supervision occurs and the likelihood that we all have undetected biases and assumptions that influence our supervisory behavior, we suggest growth in this area be an ongoing goal for supervisors. One way to address such a goal is to request feedback from a colleague or supervisor of a different gender, race, ethnicity, or sexual orientation, based on videotape review of your supervision session, live observation, or IPR. A similar approach could be used for any other factors you believe could be influencing your behavior, consciously or unconsciously, with one or more supervisees, such as age, socioeconomic status, and religious or spiritual orientation. Any activities that broaden one's multicultural awareness and enhance one's racial identity status would be beneficial. Ladany, Brittan-Powell, and Pannu (1997) found that when supervisors' racial identity was high, supervisees gave higher ratings of the supervisory working alliance and reported their supervisors had greater influence on their multicultural competence. Importantly, Ladany et al. also found that supervisees rated supervisors of color as more impactful, regardless of the supervisee's race. Thus, supervisees and supervisors likely would benefit from interacting with supervisors of color. It seems plausible that having a variety of supervisors who differ in gender, sexual orientation, and other variables, also would be preferable (Borders, 2001), although the developmental readiness of supervisees, such as their ability to handle multiple perspectives, must be considered.

Supervisee Anxiety and Resistance

A consistent theme in the supervision literature—as well as any supervisor's discussion with colleagues—is supervisee anxiety. Managing that anxiety is a major aspect of your work as a supervisor. As in any learning situation, some anxiety is helpful as a motivator for preparation, study, review, and openness to feedback. Your task is to monitor the balance of challenge and support you provide so that the counselor is willing to try new behaviors, take new perspectives, face new insights about self, or struggle with an ethical dilemma. The counselor needs to feel encouraged and supported—and pushed. The half-step mismatch described in developmental models is another way of thinking about managing a balance of challenge and support in the supervision environment (i.e., in individual and group supervision sessions as well as site expectations, client level and difficulty, etc.). Note that managing this balance not only means that you are sensitive to the need for more support; you also deliberately choose to increase the challenge—and anxiety—levels (cf. Loganbill et al., 1982). Blocher (1983) noted that "complexity, ambiguity, novelty, abstraction, and intensity" (p. 31) tend to raise the challenge level.

Supervisee anxiety, then, should not be viewed as a problem. In particular, it is not a deficiency of the supervisee. It is a normal and expected condition of any learning environment. Supervision is evaluative, there is a power differential in the relationship, and supervisees typically are quite invested, personally, in their work. For supervisees, there is a lot on the line, including their self-esteem and self-concept as a helper and as a person. Anxiety, then, is a given (Bradley & Gould, 1994).

Supervisee anxiety also is variable; the level of anxiety varies within a supervision session, across a semester, across developmental levels, by client difficulty (state anxiety). In addition, each supervisee brings his or her own predilection toward anxious behaviors and thoughts (trait anxiety). Relatedly, they also vary in how they handle failure, and even how they define it. The obvious point is that the appropriate balance of challenge and support will be highly individualized, and it will fluctuate with any one supervisee.

Your manner of challenging and supporting also will need to vary. Supervisees arrive with different cultural expectations related to confrontation and feedback, self-disclosure, and achievement. They have had different life experiences with authority figures as well as nurturing ones. They also bring different personality traits that influence how they manage their anxiety, handle challenge, and react to support (cf. Tracy, Ellickson, & Sherry, 1989). In addition, they will be influenced by life events throughout their training and supervised experiences, both positive (e.g., birth of a child) and negative (e.g., divorce), that will affect their anxiety levels, available resources for handling challenges, and supervision needs. Again, then, your choice of methods of challenging and supporting will need to be customized by supervisee.

It is worth noting that supervisors bring their own unique personal and professional histories to the relationship. We, the authors, are both Southern females, and so were well-trained to be indirect and nonconfrontive (i.e., polite). These cultural behaviors had to be revised during our counseling and supervision training experiences. Undoubtedly, they still influence our supervisory interactions. Similarly, you likely are aware of some traits, tendencies, and preferences that need to be monitored in your own supervision behavior. In particular, you may want to consider your experiences with authority figures as well as your experiences in evaluative, overseeing roles.

Resistance

A corollary of anxiety is "resistance." Supervisees necessarily must find ways to handle their anxiety, and sometimes their attempts are not productive. We resist the word *resistance*, due to its negative connotations. Nevertheless, it is a word that describes behaviors that each supervisor must face because, once again, resistance *per se* is a normal, predictable supervisee response. The degree of resistance ranges widely, and it is manifested in many individualized (and sometimes creative) ways. Given the prevalence of anxiety in supervision, then, some attention to and preparation for supervisee resistance is needed.

Liddle (1986) provided a very useful framework for examining resistant behaviors. In particular, she described resistance as a response to perceived threat rather than resistance to learning. From this perspective, supervisee resistance actually can be a necessary and functional response. Resistance may reflect the supervisee's attempt to reduce anxiety to a manageable and productive level or slow down the pace of learning (i.e., "I've had all I can handle for one day!"). Resistance also may indicate that the supervisory material is too close to some unresolved conflict or personal issue that threatens the supervisee's current level of coping with that material. Liddle also pointed out that supervisee resistance may be a reasonable response to inappropriate supervisor behavior (e.g., too rigid or dogmatic).

Resistant behaviors, then, are maladaptive coping behaviors that interfere with learning. The supervisor's appropriate response is either to reduce the threat in the supervision climate or help the supervisee find new ways of coping that do not interfere with learning. Liddle outlined a mutual problem-solving approach in which the situation is openly discussed (i.e., identify the source of anxiety and perceived threat, brainstorm ways to reduce the supervisee's experience of threat). As a part of this approach, the supervisor may need to help the supervisee apply cognitive-behavioral techniques (e.g., self-talk) for self-managing anxiety. Importantly, what creates intense perceived threat for one supervisee may have little effect on another supervisee. Thus, the assessment and intervention will need to be tailored for the particular supervisee.

Although resistant behaviors are rather idiosyncratic to the supervisee, there are some common types of behaviors that signal resistance. Supervisees, for example, may present as overly enthusiastic, self-effacing, submissive, argumentative, aloof, or forgetful during supervision (Borders & Leddick, 1987). Resistant behaviors often become evident in supervisee concerns regarding taping of counseling sessions (Goldberg, 1983). Obviously, taping (particularly videotaping and other direct observation supervision methods) increases supervisee vulnerability, as "every move in session [is] open for scrutiny" (Goodyear & Nelson, 1997, p. 336) by both the supervisor and peers in group supervision. Taping policies and requirements need to be clarified in the initial supervision session (Goldberg, 1983; Goodyear & Nelson, 1997; see also chap. 2, this volume), and supervisee concerns should be acknowledged and normalized. The more specifics the supervisor provides regarding how the tapes will be reviewed and used in supervision, the better (see also chaps. 2 and 7, this volume). Supervisors can avoid focusing on taping as a rule or mandate, and instead emphasize the rich opportunities for learning that the tapes provide, as well as how they can safeguard the client and the counselor (e.g., evidence that counselor completed a suicide assessment). Although supervisee concerns certainly may reflect fears related to taping, they also may originate in larger issues causing anxiety and resistance (e.g., issues involving authority figures). The intensity of a supervisee's protests (i.e., "but what if the client doesn't want to be taped?" vs. an insistence that taping breaks confidentiality and thus is unethical) provides clues about the degree of perceived threat, and thus the amount of energy required to help the supervisee get past the concern.

Some caricatures of resistant behaviors have been described by Kadushin (1968) as "games" that supervisees play, such as "Be nice to me because I am nice to you," "I did like I was told," "It's all so confusing," and "What you don't know won't hurt you." Importantly, Kadushin pointed out that supervisors can benefit from these games (e.g., feel flattered), and that supervisees can "play games" only if they are allowed to do so. Similarly, Hawthorne (1975) described games supervisors may set up themselves as a way of dealing with their own concerns about authority (e.g., either "they won't let me" or "I know you really can't do without me."). Rozsnafszky (1979) defined immature supervisors as those who have an unconscious need for conquest and power (e.g., teddy bear, super guru, big mother).

As these caricatures and discussions of perceived threat make clear, both supervisee and supervisor can experience transference or countertransference within the supervision relationship. (For more detailed discussions of supervisor countertransference, see Bernard & Goodyear, 1998, pp. 84–87; DeLucia-Waack, 1999; and Ladany, Constantine, Miller, Erickson, & Muse-Burke, 2000.) In particular, we suggest that you give some thought to which types of resistant behavior push your buttons the hardest, and practice your response (and keeping your cool). Relatedly, we have found that beginning supervisors, perhaps because they are dealing with their own anxiety, can take a supervisee's resistant behaviors personally. In most cases, the supervisee is not resisting you, but your behavior that creates a threat. So, step back and assess, stay objective, and try to hear the supervisee's message.

As suggested throughout this section, supervisors need to anticipate resistance and develop a wide repertoire of interventions for varying levels of resistance (Borders, 2004). A supervisor can use proactive, preventive measures in the initial session to lower the sources of anxiety (e.g., determine learning goals for supervision). Throughout the sessions, the supervisor also can phrase feedback in ways that avoid judgmental language and labeling (e.g., frame feedback in terms of learning goals; see chaps. 2, 3, and 7, this volume). When these efforts aren't enough, the supervisor will need more direct, remedial methods

Table 5.1 Three Categories of Supervisor Response to Supervisee Resistance

Preventive Measures

Purpose is to be proactive, making anxiety a part of the supervision agenda upfront.

1. Establish working contract for supervision.
2. Anticipate and normalize anxiety.
3. Determine learning goals for supervision.
4. Conduct group supervision.

Guidelines for Giving Feedback

Purpose is to avoid making global judgments and labeling, so that the supervisee doesn't hear personal criticism.

1. Frame feedback in terms of learning goals.
2. Make specific, concrete statements about counselor behavior.
3. Identify client's response to counselor behavior.
4. Suggest alternative behaviors.
5. Help counselor prepare to change behavior.
6. State supervision goals positively.
7. Base goal attainment on *attempting* new behavior rather than *perfection.*
8. Point out small steps toward goals.
9. Help supervisee identify assets, resources, positive behaviors and attitudes they can use to make changes.
10. Use supervision interventions that take you out of the "expert" role.
11. Use the think-aloud approach.
12. Give feedback in the form of a metaphor for client, counselor, or counseling relationship.

Remedial Methods

Purpose is to deal more directly with resistance that is resistant to other interventions.

1. Ignore.
2. Use humor (nonsarcastic).
3. Identify irrational beliefs or dysfunctional thoughts.
4. Focus on underlying issues.
5. Use Columbo technique.
6. Use confrontation.
7. Use purposeful self-disclosure.
8. Use nondefensive interpretation.
9. Use nondefensive immediacy statements about the supervisory relationship and process.
10. Use a metaphor for the supervisory relationship.
11. Use IPR.
12. Use paradoxical intervention.

Source: Borders, L. D. (2004). *Anxiety and resistance: Dealing with challenges of skill and patience.* Manuscript in preparation.

to address the resistance. Table 5.1 provides some suggested methods in each of these categories (see also Masters, 1992).

As implied here and in other chapters of this book, the supervisor needs to take the lead in identifying anxiety, resistance, and other conflicts in the supervisory relationship. The supervisor needs to be open to discussion of these situations, including, potentially, how the supervisor herself is contributing to the conflict. And the supervisor needs to develop the skills for moving through these difficulties and impasses. Unresolved conflicts have substantial negative effects not only on the supervisory relationship, but also on the supervisee's well-being and therapeutic effectiveness (Gray, Ladany, Walker, & Ancis, 2001; Nelson & Friedlander, 2001).

We offer three final, brief notes to this section. First, supervisors, especially new supervisors, necessarily have their own sources of anxiety, including performance anxiety, feelings about authority and evaluation, and concerns about legal and ethical responsibilities. It is important to acknowledge these; identify how these are manifested in your behaviors, thoughts, emotions, and even your body (i.e., the knotted stomach); and prearrange methods for handling these, including support of supervisors, peers, and friends outside the supervision setting. Second, how you react (affectively) and respond (behaviorally) to a resistant supervisee is powerful modeling. Your response is instructive to the supervisee of how he can respond to the (inevitable) resistant client. In fact, you may observe your behavior in your supervisee's next tape. In other words, the supervisory relationship itself often is the vehicle for learning, even if unintentionally. Finally, a sense of humor will take you (and your supervisees) a long way. It may be particularly helpful to hold onto it when dealing with anxiety and resistance in supervision.

Parallel Process

Parallel process is perhaps the most unique dynamic in supervision. Our supervision students always find it fascinating. Here again, the supervision relationship itself is a vehicle for learning. In other words, the supervisor-supervisee interaction, the process of supervision, is the teaching medium.

Historically, parallel process is rooted in concepts of psychoanalytic theory, including transference and countertransference, introjection and projection. Searles (1955) described "the reflection process" in which "the processes at work currently in the *relationship between* patient and therapist are often reflected in the *relationship between* therapist and supervisor" (p. 135). According to Searles, the process begins with the counselor's unconscious identification with the client. Essentially, (1) the client becomes anxious or defensive when unresolved material gets close to awareness; (2) the counselor intuitively experiences the client's anxiety as well as the defense against it; (3) due to her own anxiety, the counselor also is unable to get close to and articulate the client's critical material; (4) the counselor acts out the anxiety and defense in supervision; and (5) the supervisor experiences an emotional response similar to what the counselor and client are experiencing. It is up to the supervisor to interrupt the spiraling reflection and help the counselor articulate and then work through the client's block. A simple example may make this clearer (see also Searles, 1955):

> A panicked client demands the counselor tell him what to do; caught up in the client's affect, the overwhelmed counselor turns to the supervisor for a quick solution to the client's dilemma. In response to the counselor's behavior, the supervisor feels an urgent need to take over or provide an answer. The supervisor who is alert to the reflection process, however, can interrupt the spiraling affective reactions and, instead, point out the message the client seems to be trying to convey through his behavior. (Borders & Leddick, 1987, pp. 44–45)

Given the psychoanalytic context of Searles' (1955) writing, an important point for him was that the counselor's behavior in the supervision session was not a manifestation of the counselor's own unresolved psychodynamic issues. Over the years, that distinction has become less central, and the definition of parallel process has broadened. In addition to the client, the origin of the parallel process now also may be the counselor or the supervisor, and may or may not be rooted in classic psychodynamic constructs. Friedman (1983) described an example of parallel process that was rooted in the counselor's countertransference reactions to the client. Later, McNeill and Worthen (1989) provided two case illustrations in which the parallel process resulted from a counselor's discomfort with confrontation (in counseling and supervision), and a counselor's desire to be respected and liked (by both the supervisor and the client).

Doehrman (1976) found evidence for what Ekstein and Wallerstein (1972) termed *reverse parallelism*. Doehrman followed two supervisors, four student therapists, and eight patients at a psychology clinic for 20 weeks. She found that all four therapists "played supervisor with their patients" (p. 81), in that they behaved with patients in similar or opposite ways that they perceived their supervisors behaving with them. The parallels included both positive and negative behaviors. Importantly, resolution of the transference impasses in the supervisory relationships led to resolution of the transference binds in the therapeutic relationships. In essence, Doehrman noted, the supervisors modeled ways the therapists "could intervene more constructively and therapeutically in the interpersonal binds that limited the progress of their therapies" (p. 78). In addition, she observed parallel behaviors in the therapists' relationships with other supervisors, their own therapists, and even the researcher herself. Martin, Goodyear, and Newton (1987) speculated about unexpected evidence of a similar process in a case study. The supervisor's frustration with one supervisee seemed to have intruded on his work with a second supervisee. Thus, Martin et al. suggested, dynamics at work in one supervision relationship could transfer over to, or be paralleled in, another supervision relationship.

Similarly, Stoltenberg and Delworth (1987) speculated that a parallel process could occur when an advanced counseling student was supervising a beginning counselor, in that the advanced student-supervisor might parallel an issue or behavior from her own supervision in working with the beginning counselor, supervising as she was being supervised. Indeed, this dynamic can be used intentionally by the supervisor of supervision. One of us supervised a beginning supervisor who reported she was bored with an intern's work because the counseling sessions "go nowhere." Similarly, the supervision sessions were unfocused, wandering from topic to topic with no real connection or purpose. As an intervention (metamodeling, if you will), the supervision of supervision session was structured deliberately, beginning with a statement of the agenda for the session and how it would be structured. Within the first one third of the session, the beginning supervisor commented on the structure and added, "This is what I need to do with the intern—*and* what she needs to do with her clients!" The supervisor was complimented on her insight, with no mention of the deliberate intervention.

There have been some differences of opinion about how a supervisor should handle parallel process dynamics in supervision (Bernard & Goodyear, 1998; Sumerel, 1994). Currently, the general consensus is that addressing parallel process issues directly with a beginning-level counselor probably would be more confusing than productive. As the developmental models suggest, these counselors are focused on skill development for the most part, and are not ready to deal with more complex interpersonal dynamics such as transference and countertransference. Most supervision professionals (e.g., McNeill & Worthen, 1989; Neufeldt et al., 1995), then, suggest that any interventions with beginners regarding a parallel process dynamic be indirect, simple, and concrete, dealing directly with the supervisee's feelings without pointing out or interpreting the parallel process in the supervision session (see e.g., McNeill & Worthen, 1989, p. 332, and Neufeldt et al., pp. 76–77). In essence the supervisor models how the counselor can respond to the client.

More advanced supervisees are more open to, and even welcome, attention to the complex dynamics involved in parallel process and are more willing to examine directly their feelings and reactions during counseling and supervision. Thus, with these supervisees an interpretation of the parallel process phenomenon is more appropriate and more likely to be constructive. Nevertheless, McNeill and Worthen (1989) cautioned that ongoing attention to parallel process and the supervision relationship can be too much of a good thing, and reminded us that timing of such interventions is a key to their effectiveness. When the supervision feels "stuck," this may be a signal that some consideration of parallel process would be instructive.

Summary

We hope we have adequately described and illustrated the pivotal power of the supervision relationship. We also hope it is clear that this working relationship will not always be rosy and pleasant. Indeed, the frustrating, confusing, and even maddening times may be your greatest opportunities to facilitate supervisee insight and growth. As Doehrman (1976) noted, "tension in the supervisory relationship is inevitable; when understood and handled skillfully, it is instrumental in the therapist's growth" (p. 78)—and the supervisor's growth.

Discussion Questions

1. What theoretical models and constructs and beliefs do you draw from to understand the supervisory relationship? How are these helpful? How might they be limiting?
2. Discuss the interplay of power and involvement in the supervisory relationship.
3. What kinds of power do you have, personally and professionally, that you bring to the supervisory relationship?
4. As suggested earlier in the chapter, consider your experiences with authority figures (e.g., how did you respond to critical feedback?) and your experiences in authority roles (e.g., how comfortable were you in providing evaluative feedback?).
5. Which caricatures of resistant behaviors have you observed in supervisees? Which caricatures of supervisors might you be vulnerable to?
6. Consider a recent supervision experience and consider how parallel process may have been at work in that experience. What would be the appropriate way to address this parallel process, given the developmental level of the supervisee?
7. Stuart, a White male in his late thirties, married with children, comes under your supervision as a new employee at your agency. He is an LPC with 10 years of clinical experience, some of that "supervised" (using a staffing model, not developmental supervision). You have found that Stuart tends to be emotional in his approach to clients, sometimes overstepping boundaries by making home visits and allowing parents to use him as a mouthpiece for disciplining their children (his clients). He also seems overly sure of himself and his skills, to the point of personalizing your developmentally appropriate constructive criticism. Early in the supervisory relationship, Stuart appeared too scared of your supervision to respond honestly. Then, after your initial tape review, he accused you of not liking him and attacking his skills and abilities.

    a. This session could become a pivotal one in the relationship. Explain how you would respond to Stuart's anxiety in order to best support the supervisory relationship.
    b. What might you learn from this experience that could help you determine the best balance between challenge and support for this supervisee?

8. You are supervising Caty, a single White female in her early twenties, who appears to be highly capable and intelligent, yet very nervous about her performance in her first practicum experience. Living with her parents and dealing with a family illness during the semester has added to her stress level. Because of her education background (student teaching), Caty feels most comfortable working with groups, especially large groups. She was placed in a high school, where some clients are only 4 to 5 years younger than she is, and this has made it difficult for her to separate, especially in individual counseling with female clients. She feels particularly stuck with one female client, a student new to the school who is also experiencing family illness and having adjustment difficulties. Some of Caty's other concerns include questioning her own judgment in-session, difficulty setting parameters of the counseling relationship, and discomfort with confronting clients.

    a. What is the major issue Caty faces?
    b. How can you best address this (and other) issue(s) in the most developmentally appropriate ways?

Chapter 6

Ethical Issues in Supervision

A major advancement for the profession of counseling supervision in the area of legal and ethical considerations occurred in 1993, when the ACES Executive Council endorsed the Ethical Guidelines for Counseling Supervisors (Hart, Borders, Nance, & Paradise, 1995; see Appendix C, this volume). Originally created and recommended by the ACES Supervision Interest Network, these guidelines were the first formalized set of ethical standards developed solely with the counselor educator or counseling supervisor in mind. Although ACES currently does not review complaints regarding alleged noncompliance with these guidelines, the association offers the 1993 document as a means to assist counseling supervisors in their everyday practice of supervision.

As always, along with ethical issues come legal considerations, although the two are not always in agreement (i.e., you might be acting ethically and still break the law, and vice versa). In today's litigious society, professionals must always remain cognizant of legal liability concerns. However, we challenge you to look beyond the letter of the law to the spirit of ethical responsibility—to your supervisees, your supervisees' clients, and your profession. Fortunately, you have the Ethical Guidelines for Counseling Supervisors to rely on when making ethical decisions within your supervision practice.

The following list of issues represents special ethical concerns in counseling supervision. As a professional counselor, you are probably used to thinking about most of these issues as they relate to your work with clients, and relying on the ACA ethical standards in that regard. We now discuss each issue as it pertains to the process of counseling supervision, referring you to the ACES Ethical Guidelines when appropriate. As a counseling supervisor, you will need to keep both sets of standards in mind because you are often simultaneously responsible for the growth of both the supervisee and the client.

Dual Roles

According to Corey, Corey, and Callanan (1998) *dual roles* can be defined as the combination of distinct relationship roles wherein the professional role or even one's professional judgment might become impaired. Because of the

DOI: 10.4324/9781003251583-6

uniquely intimate nature of the supervisory relationship, as well as the likely vulnerability of the supervisee, dual role issues in supervision are practically unavoidable. It is up to you, as the supervisor, to monitor these possible dual roles in order to deter impairment to the relationship or harm to the supervisee (Bernard & Goodyear, 1998; Maki & Bernard, 2003).

There are three possible types of dual roles: social, sexual, and therapeutic. In many cases, especially for university supervisors, the overlapping of social roles is almost impossible to avoid. You may teach your supervisee in a class, serve as her academic advisor, and work as the internship placement coordinator involved in gathering and approving her application for a particular site. As long as you clearly explain the differences among these roles, you should be able to appropriately minimize any conflicts these multiple roles might induce (see Appendix C, Guideline 2.09, this volume). Given that you often have many things in common with your supervisees, it also quite possible that you may develop a personal friendship. The important thing to remember is that supervisors need to refrain from any form of social interaction which might lead to a loss of objectivity regarding their supervisees' skills and abilities (see Appendix C, Guideline 2.10, this volume). Both the supervisor and the supervisee must always keep in mind that this is an evaluative relationship, one focused on promoting the personal and professional growth of the supervisee. Anything that might cause the supervisor to be less confrontive or challenging would only impede the supervisee's professional growth (Baltimore, Crutchfield, Gillam, & Lee, 2001).

The dual role that should be avoided at all costs is that of a sexual relationship between supervisor and supervisee (see Appendix C, Guideline 2.10, this volume). Sexual attraction may or may not be a transference or countertransference reaction to a supervisee. Given similarities in interests, values, and sometimes age, just as with feelings of friendship, genuine sexual attraction may occur. In fact, we would go as far as to say that if you think you will never be attracted to a supervisee, you likely are kidding yourself. Of course, feeling attracted and acting on that attraction are two different things. If you should have more than typical positive feelings about your supervisee (e.g., sexual fantasies, seductive behavior, unwarranted physical contact, etc.), action is needed to determine the origin of those feelings and then work toward learning from them (i.e., the source of the transference or countertransference). If, after examination within a supervision session, you and your supervisee determine that the sexual attraction is genuine, then you must decide on the best way to avoid this type of dual relationship. In some cases, this might mean relinquishing your supervisory role.

Therapeutic dual roles are unique to supervision. Because personal issues (as they relate to the professional growth of the supervisee) often are addressed in counseling supervision, this can become a slippery slope (Baltimore et al., 2001). When you were a professional counselor, your appropriate role with your client was a therapeutic one. As you begin to function as a counseling supervisor, there will be times when you react to your supervisee as a counselor might react to a client. Use of your counseling skills within the supervisory relationship can be totally appropriate when encouraging supervisee self-awareness as a means of impacting professional functioning. However, you must be on your guard against allowing the relationship to become more therapeutic than supervisory (see Appendix C, Guideline 2.11, this volume). We tell our supervisees early in our interactions that we are not there to provide them with counseling (as we have found that some supervisees are seeking just that or think this is appropriate). This type of boundary delineation up front will help prevent the supervision from coming closer to therapy for the supervisee than is appropriate (see also chap. 2, this volume).

Competence

As a supervisor, you are obviously responsible for addressing the counseling competency level of your supervisee. That is what supervision is all about. In this section, we address your ethical responsibilities for your own competence as a counseling supervisor. Why would we presume to supervise counselors working with a particular population if we had not had training and/or experience with that client population ourselves? It would be wise to supervise only in your areas of clinical competence and experience (see Appendix C, Guideline 3.02, this volume).

The profession of counseling supervision is still a relatively young one; the Approved Clinical Supervisor (ACS) credential was established by the National Board of Certified Counselors (NBCC) in 1998. This means that there are still common expectations that, if you are a competent counselor, you also should be able to supervise. However, without systematic knowledge regarding the process of supervision, you are as likely to do harm as to do good for your supervisees. We suggest you have some formal training in supervision before initiating your role as a counseling supervisor (see Appendix C, Guideline 2.01, this volume). This training could take the form of university courses, seminars, or professional conference presentations. Ideally, your training in supervision would also include some type of supervised supervision experience, so that you have gained some actual supervision practice in a safe learning environment.

An additional responsibility of the supervisor is that of continuing with your own personal and professional development. Just as you did as a professional counselor, you will want to continue seeking additional training to update your skills constantly. We recommend you pursue activities that include both counseling and supervision topics (see Appendix C, Guideline 2.02, this volume), as both will be salient to your supervision practice. This type of ongoing professional development also allows you to continue to network with your professional peers.

Consultation

A supervisor cannot successfully exist in a vacuum, and should proactively avoid professional isolation. One means of doing so was mentioned previously—seeking continued professional development opportunities. An additional means of preventing isolation is to seek consultation from your fellow supervisors (Maki & Bernard, 2003). You may want to consult with peers on a regular basis in order to achieve and maintain quality in counselor training and supervision (see Appendix C, Guideline 3.03, this volume).

Consulting with peers will help you maintain your objectivity when a supervisory issue has you feeling stuck or frustrated with a supervisee. Your peer's different perspective can provide you with a clearer picture of what might be going on, and help you think about your supervisee in a new way. Perhaps you are working with a supervisee on a complex client case, and feel the need to bring in some fresh ideas on the topic. Opening the case up to multiple perspectives through consultation can inject new life into your ability to help your supervisee perform (Baltimore et al., 2001).

Consultation also might take the form of structured peer supervision of supervision. Having briefly been a part of one such peer supervision group, the second author can attest that it helped each of us address the training needs of our supervisees more effectively and efficiently. This regular interaction served the additional purpose of increasing our own particular supervisory skills, as we brought specific issues (via taped supervision sessions) to the group for critical feedback.

Informed Consent

Your supervisory responsibilities regarding informed consent are twofold. You must address the client's right to be informed about the process of supervision, as well as the supervisee's right to know about conditions and responsibilities involved in the supervisory process. When supervising novice counselors especially, we suggest you also be clear about the client's right to informed consent within the counseling process (i.e., the goals and purposes of counseling, and the risks and benefits of service). As the supervisee informs the client of his right to confidentiality, have her inform the client that she is a counselor-in-training who is receiving counseling supervision, that their counseling sessions may be observed or taped for educational or supervisory purposes, and that she may also be discussing the client's case in supervision (see Appendix C, Guideline 1.01, this volume). In addition, the client has the right to be informed of the confidential nature of the supervisory relationship, and must be assured that his right to confidentiality will not be violated (see Appendix C, Guideline 1.03, this volume).

During your initial supervision session, it is important to clearly inform your supervisee of the parameters of the supervisory process (Bernard &

Goodyear, 1998). For the university supervisor, most of the policies and procedures will be spelled out in a syllabus for the practicum or internship being supervised. If you are a supervisor in private practice this information can be provided in the form of a professional disclosure statement and contract (Cobia & Boes, 2000). Early in the supervisory relationship, you may want to discuss with supervisees your professional training and experiences, your theoretical orientation to counseling, and the model of supervision you will be utilizing with them (see Appendix C, Guideline 3.03, this volume). Your supervisee has the right to know how you will be documenting the supervision, what you expect of him as a supervisee, and what he can expect of you as a supervisor (see chap. 2, this volume, for further details).

Due Process

The informed supervisor certainly will be familiar with due process, a legal concept that allows individuals to expect certain rights and liberties within a given situation. As a supervisor, you are responsible for ensuring that your supervisee is familiar with the training objectives of supervision, the assessment procedures and criteria for evaluation, the parameters of supervision, and your expectations regarding personal growth activities and self-reflection. Once you have communicated with your supervisee on these topics, we recommend that you also provide regular evaluative feedback to the supervisee, allowing her ample time to work toward improving any skills you may find lacking.

The most egregious violation of a supervisee's due process would be a negative summative evaluation or dismissal from a training program without prior warning or appropriate time for the supervisee to work toward improvement (see Appendix C, Guideline 2.13, this volume).

Evaluation

In order to ensure the most positive growth experience possible for your supervisees, continuous feedback, both critical and supportive is necessary (see Appendix C, Guideline 2.08, this volume). Meeting face-to-face with your supervisees on a regular basis, so that you may review and discuss actual work samples (see Appendix C, Guidelines 2.06 and 2.07, this volume), is crucial to providing constructive feedback. Through ongoing formative evaluations, you help supervisees work toward specific goals, so that their summative evaluations (at the termination of the supervisory relationship) can be positive (see chap. 7, this volume, for a discussion of evaluation and feedback issues). Feedback should be given both orally and in written form and should be used to provide your supervisees with information regarding any personal and professional limitations you have observed, which, in your professional opinion, might impair their abilities to provide adequate counseling services.

Equally important to ethical evaluation is maintaining regular notes on your supervision sessions (see also chap. 7, this volume). By documenting what transpired in your supervisory meetings, you will be able to provide a clear and thorough written summative evaluation at the end of the supervisory experience. This type of documentation will also show that you are conducting your supervision in a professionally responsible manner, and help you legally account for your actions within each supervision session, should that be necessary. In the case of consultation with other counseling supervisors, you would also need to document any information shared and recommendations taken or acted upon. Keeping thorough supervision notes may seen time consuming, but it will definitely be worth it in the long run.

Vicarious Liability

A counseling supervisor can be held legally liable for any negligent behavior by the supervisee that occurs during the course of the supervisory relationship. The legal term for this type of vicarious liability is *Respondeat Superior*. The law says that you have an obligation to check in with your supervisees to make sure that they are doing what you have required of them (Benshoff, Borders, & Daniel, 2001). The higher level of control you have over your supervisees, the more likely it is that you will be held legally liable (e.g., students, volunteers, and employees are under an onsite supervisor's control much more so than practitioners seeking licensure are under the control of a private practice counseling supervisor). This is the scary aspect of supervision, and one reason that many counseling practitioners shy away from the profession of counseling supervision.

There are numerous ways to limit your supervisory liability. To begin, it is imperative that you acquire and maintain professional liability insurance that covers your work within the counseling supervisor's role. You also will want to clearly define the goals and parameters of the supervisory relationship within some type of written agreement, signed by both the supervisor and the supervisee, then avoid extending the limits of your liability unnecessarily (see Benshoff et al., 2001). Always consult with colleagues under any questionable supervisory circumstances, and, if possible and appropriate, involve administrative superiors in ethical and legal decision making.

Discussion Questions

1. Of the supervisees you currently supervise (or anticipate supervising), who present the potential for dual relationships? How might these multiple roles affect your supervisory relationship? How do you think this could best be handled?
2. Read through informed consent documents used with clients at your current site. Do they adequately inform clients of any supervision of their counselor? If not, what changes need to be made in the wording?

3. Sharon, an African-American school counseling intern, has been quiet and somewhat unresponsive in your supervision group. In your individual supervision sessions, she seems disinterested, often having to reschedule because she hasn't been able to make a counseling session tape for your review. Midway through the semester, her site supervisor contacts you to inform you that Sharon has not been to the site for the last 3 days, nor has she made any contact with the site supervisor. During this discussion with the site supervisor, you learn that Sharon had some similar difficulties at the site last semester, during her practicum. You set up a meeting with the site supervisor and make several attempts to contact Sharon about attending this meeting as well. After 2 days, she remains unresponsive and fails to either contact you or the site supervisor or attend the meeting.
   a. What are the ethical issues involved here?
   b. As a gatekeeper for the counseling profession, how could you most responsibly deal with this ethical dilemma?

Chapter 7

Evaluation of the Supervisee

Although many of us are loath to admit it, evaluation truly lies at the heart of counseling supervision. In fact, "because we are always communicating, an evaluative message can always be inferred" (Bernard & Goodyear, 1998, p. 153). As a supervisor, you are a gatekeeper to the counseling profession, and it is your assessment and evaluation of your supervisees' counseling skills and abilities that allow you to determine who should or should not become future counseling practitioners. This responsibility, coupled with the legal liability supervisors also might face, may well give you pause. After all, you were initially trained as a counselor, a professional practiced in avoiding judgment of your clients, allowing your clients to determine their own therapeutic goals rather than imposing your own goals upon them. No wonder most beginning supervisors feel uncomfortable with the evaluative component of counseling supervision.

Of course, without feedback and evaluation, how will the supervisee learn and grow as a counselor? Not only is it your ethical responsibility to provide supervisory feedback and evaluation, it is also something most supervisees desire from you as well. Inevitably, in our initial supervision sessions, when we ask supervisees what they hope to get from the supervisory process, they request constructive feedback on their counseling skills. If nothing else, they want us to tell them how to do it right!

Importance of a Positive Environment in Supervision

In chapter 2 (this volume), you learned how to begin the supervision process by clearly explaining the parameters of supervision to your supervisee. Once this mutual understanding is established and supervisees become aware of the structure and expectations involved in the process, they will feel less vulnerable and more open to receiving your feedback. In the face of persisting supervisee defensiveness, you would do well to examine the environment you are providing during your supervision sessions. Is it

DOI: 10.4324/9781003251583-7

positive, accepting, supportive, respectful, and appropriately challenging, or is it possibly being perceived by the supervisee as a more judgmental and threatening environment? In order to decrease that early defensiveness, you may need to directly discuss it with the supervisee (see also chap. 5, this volume).

Careful goal setting and timely feedback increase supervisees' satisfaction with supervision (Lehrman-Waterman & Ladany, 2001). Setting learning goals in collaboration with the supervisee allows the two of you the opportunity to jointly examine the supervisee's strengths and weaknesses. What does the supervisee know about himself or herself as a counselor? What skills might he or she already have identified as needing improvement? Supervisees also need to hear that these learning goals are never set in stone and may be revised throughout the supervisory process. It is important for the two of you to go through this process together, and end it by agreeing that both of you will be evaluating the supervisee based on movement toward achieving these goals. It is also crucial to be clear about your own goals for supervisees so that they understand the issues and skills on which they will be evaluated. Take care to communicate your respect for your supervisees, so that they can more easily trust you and therefore bring their questions and issues to you in session.

There are bound to be factors of both similarity and dissimilarity between you and your supervisee, many of which can influence your supervisory evaluation. How will you react, for example, if you have a supervisee who is 15 years older than you? Could this factor induce some hesitancy on your part to give the supervisee critical feedback? What if the two of you have similar outside interests and find yourselves attending community meetings of the same mountain biking club? Might this added social interaction have an impact on your ability to objectively assess and address your supervisee's skills and abilities? Likewise, if you have previously taught the supervisee in class, this prior association could impact upon your objectivity, in either a positive or a negative direction. We have a tendency to hold on to our initial impressions of our supervisees, and are more likely to trust our negative impressions more than our positive ones. In other words, you may question your own objectivity if you are aware that this was an excellent student in class, but if the supervisee made an earlier negative impression on you, you are likely to evaluate more harshly. Keep in mind that we all have a bad day once in a while, even supervisors!

The environment you set for the beginning few supervision sessions will go a long way in establishing a positive working relationship in supervision. Although dynamics may shift and change throughout the course of supervision, as the supervisor, it remains your responsibility to maintain this positive learning environment. You know that feedback and evaluation are not synonymous with criticism, which usually holds a more negative connotation. Remember, you are not there to criticize your supervisees but to help them learn as much as possible about who they are as a counselor.

Giving Critical Feedback: Balancing Challenge and Support

Within a positive learning environment, in a trusting supervisory relationship, your supervisees will better hear your critical feedback. It is your responsibility to clearly communicate to your supervisees about how and when you will give them feedback about their counseling practice. All supervisees need to hear supportive comments about their work—we all want to know when we are doing something well! Likewise, challenging feedback regarding skills or techniques the supervisees need to improve remains crucial to their personal and professional growth. The ratio of challenge to support, however, will vary depending on the supervisee's developmental level, needs and personality, and self-perceptions of abilities and skills (see also chap. 5, this volume).

As the supervisor, you set the stage for the action that occurs during the supervision session. Your expectations and demands of your supervisees can communicate to them what they might expect within each session. Your review of tapes prior to your sessions, for instance, tells supervisees to expect regular feedback regarding their activities during each taped counseling session. We have found that the more regularly (and often) supervisory feedback is offered, the more quickly it becomes welcomed and appreciated by the supervisee.

Formative Evaluations

Of the two types of evaluation utilized in supervision (formative and summative), it is the regular, consistent formative evaluations that are most likely to be communicated verbally. As the supervisor, you are constantly assessing your supervisee on any number of skills, abilities, and cognitions. In each supervision session, your job is to choose among these assessments to formulate the most appropriate feedback to give the supervisee at any given moment. Formative evaluations can be as focused as the tentative critical statements you make about the supervisee's performance of a particular counseling technique, or as far-reaching as an interactive discussion of his case conceptualization of the client.

The key to giving successful formative feedback is the regularity with which it is presented. If you were to review and critique only one counseling tape during a 6-month supervisory relationship, imagine how anxious your supervisee would be on the day he or she was to receive your feedback! It would be somewhat overwhelming, not knowing how you might respond to his or her hard work. On the other hand, reviewing and discussing a counseling tape every time you have a supervision session allows supervisees to work through their anxiety with the first tape, making for much more productive sessions after that. Once your supervisees realize you're not going to berate them for every little mistake or completely rip apart their entire approach to the counseling session, they will come to supervision more curious about, and eager to receive, your expected feedback.

Looking back at your supervisees' learning goals, requiring them to provide you with case notes along with the tape, and having them list a few specific questions for supervision regarding the taped counseling session are all means of preparing yourself for giving effective feedback within each supervision session. Having all of this written documentation of the supervisees' concerns, perceptions, and ideas allows you to give specific concrete feedback on the particular things they commented on or even asked about. When you can refer to a specific question that supervisees asked you to address, they are more likely to be receptive to your comments, questions, or suggestions. (See additional suggestions for providing effective feedback in Table 5.1 and chap. 5, this volume.)

In our experience, the most successful formative feedback is that which is presented in a tentative fashion and stated as an opinion rather than a fact. For example, "It seems to me that you may have been a little too timid with your client in this session. Are you feeling like you might be able to challenge him a little more next time?" Using tentative statements reduces supervisee anxiety by allowing your supervisees the opportunity to disagree or correct you if they see fit. Asking "the right question at the right time" (Borders, 2001, p. 426) is an additional means of providing feedback in a tentative manner, one that can often stir the most productive of cognitive processes for the supervisee. In the end, what you are working toward should be a comfort level that allows your supervisees to truly consider your feedback in an open, self-reflective manner and discuss their alternatives with you in the supervision session.

Supervisory "Case Notes"

Along with the regular formative evaluative feedback you give your supervisees, as a supervisor you are also responsible for the written documentation of your supervision sessions. Different supervisors will want to keep these supervision notes in their own ways, just as different counselors find their own best means of recording the substance of each of their counseling sessions with clients. Depending on the supervisor's general approach to supervision, supervisory "case notes" might be more focused on the discussions of particular clients, or at the other extreme, mostly documenting the developmental changes the supervisee experiences. In any event, there are certain basic items that should be included each time, including name of supervisee, date and time of supervision meeting, plans for the supervision session, and types of feedback given or interventions utilized (see Fall & Sutton, 2004, and Falvey, Caldwell, & Cohen, 2002, for specific examples and sample forms).

Maintaining regular supervision notes allows the supervisor to look back at the development of supervisees over time. This will prove to be invaluable when it comes time to give supervisees a final written summative evaluation of their progress.

Peer Evaluations

All counseling supervisors are ethically bound to help their supervisees learn how to better evaluate themselves as well as how to give and receive appropriate evaluative feedback with their peers (Hart et al., 1995). One excellent means of addressing this is through the use of peer evaluations. During group supervision, peers should be encouraged, or possibly even required, to provide appropriate critical feedback to one another. We also have found it helpful and challenging to ask peers to review each other's counseling tapes regularly (along with any tape review forms and case notes for the session), and then exchange critical feedback. Although this could most easily be done in written form, it is often more effective to have them give each other the verbal feedback face to face. In a university setting, this could be done in a dyadic supervision session, with the university supervisor present as well. While the supervisees evaluate each other, the supervisor is also able to assess each supervisee's skills in giving and receiving peer feedback.

We are constantly amazed by the insights supervisees regularly gain from the feedback of their peers. Similarly, supervisees often can see and hear issues in peers' tapes that are harder to see and hear in their own session tapes. If structured appropriately in order to reduce supervisee anxiety, peer evaluations can benefit everyone involved through the use of multiple perspectives and sources of feedback.

Supervisee Self-Evaluations

As mentioned earlier, the supervisee should understand from the beginning that she will be expected to complete a self-evaluation at the end of the supervisory experience. One way to structure this self-evaluation for the supervisee is to ask her to reflect on her learning goals and describe the progress she has made toward achieving each goal. In addition, she should be able to articulate the other important things she has learned about herself as a professional counselor, and summarily evaluate her supervision experience. Requiring your supervisees to give you a final narrative, self-reflective evaluation forces them to review the supervision experience in its entirety, and synthesize the various aspects of their growth process.

In addition, you might want to ask supervisees to rate themselves using some form or assessment scale, then bring this form to the final evaluation session. Many universities have developed forms specific to their practicum or internship experience, solely for this purpose.

Supervisee's Feedback for Supervisor

One way to constantly monitor and improve your supervisory relationships is to ask your supervisees to provide you with feedback on your supervision. This can be done informally throughout the supervision experience to gain formative feedback to which you can immediately respond. It can also be summative, perhaps a form with a Likert scale, rating your supervisory effectiveness. This type of summative evaluation could be discussed during your final supervisory session, keeping in mind that it should be made as confidential as possible. We usually give our supervisees the choice of whether or not they will discuss their summative evaluation with us in the final session. If they choose to discuss it, we save it for last, so that we have given them our final evaluation prior to hearing their evaluation of us.

Summative Evaluations

The final step in any supervision experience is the supervisor's summative evaluation. This is the result of all the regular formative evaluations along the way, an articulation of the supervisor's perceptions of the supervisee's personal and professional development throughout their supervision. Your summative evaluations should be based on the criteria you outlined for your supervisee early in the supervisory process and should always be presented in written form, as well as verbally face to face. In a university setting, the summative evaluation should also address the supervisee's grade for the semester.

Your final evaluation may be a written narrative, or you may use a standard (usually self-developed) form. Often, in the university setting, both are utilized (see Table 7.1 and Table 7.2 for examples of these types of forms). We have found that providing our supervisees with a copy of a narrative summative evaluation provides a satisfying kind of closure for their supervision experience.

Discussion Questions

1. What are you currently doing in your initial supervision sessions to lay the groundwork for more effective feedback throughout the process? What

Table 7.1 Practicum Counselor Evaluation Form

Counselor: ______________________ Mid-term Evaluation: ____________________

Semester: _______________________ Final Evaluation: __________________________

Evaluate each skill area using a scale of 1 (lowest) to 5 (highest).

I. Counseling Skills	1	2	3	4	5
A. Facilitative skills	1	2	3	4	5
B. Techniques and interventions	1	2	3	4	5
1. Performance	1	2	3	4	5
2. Rationale for choice	1	2	3	4	5
C. Intake sessions	1	2	3	4	5
D. Closure sessions	1	2	3	4	5
E. Ability to respond to variety of emotions of client	1	2	3	4	5
F. Process skills (e.g., pacing, dealing with client resistance)	1	2	3	4	5
G. Variety of approaches, creativity (cognitive, affective and behavioral approaches)	1	2	3	4	5
H. Growth/Change in skills	1	2	3	4	5
I. Uses assessment instruments/results appropriately	1	2	3	4	5
Comments:					
II. Case Conceptualization	1	2	3	4	5
A. Complete, holistic assessment of client—considers background/demographic/cultural information, environmental factors (stressors and resources), cognitive, affective, and behavioral (including interpersonal) aspects of client	1	2	3	4	5
B. Integration and synthesis of above aspects to identify patterns and themes	1	2	3	4	5
C. Uses above as a basis for planning sessions, choosing interventions, setting goals	1	2	3	4	5
Comments:					
III. Self-awareness	1	2	3	4	5
A. Willingness to explore self	1	2	3	4	5
B. Uses reactions to clients appropriately/therapeutically	1	2	3	4	5
C. Avoids imposing beliefs/values on clients	1	2	3	4	5
D. Sensitive to multicultural dynamics	1	2	3	4	5
E. Able to manage transference and countertransference	1	2	3	4	5

F. Emotional stability	1	2	3	4	5
Comments:					
IV. Professional Behaviors	1	2	3	4	5
A. Paper work (case notes, treatment plans, final reports)	1	2	3	4	5
B. Onsite behaviors (e.g., is on time, dresses appropriately observes emergency protocols, etc.)	1	2	3	4	5
C. Follows ethical and legal guidelines	1	2	3	4	5
Comments:					
V. Supervision Behaviors	1	2	3	4	5
A. Self-critique (includes strengths *and* areas for improvement)	1	2	3	4	5
B. Receptive to feedback from supervisor and peers	1	2	3	4	5
C. Peer supervision (e.g., gives constructive feedback and suggestions)	1	2	3	4	5
D. Presentation of videotapes (evidence of preparation)	1	2	3	4	5
Comments:					
Practicum Counselor Date			Practicum Supervisor	Date	

might you need to do differently to positively impact your supervisee's openness to feedback?

2. Consider your current (or potential future) supervisees' similarities and dissimilarities to you. What are some ways you can maintain awareness of these factors so that your objectivity is not undermined?
3. Harry, a White male supervisee in his mid-twenties, was in his first practicum in a school setting. He had an undergraduate psychology background, appeared highly capable and intelligent, intuitive and creative. His basic skills were strong and he developed excellent rapport with the children but had some difficulty with setting goals for counseling and keeping clients on track to work on those goals. Harry's supervisor had taught him in an academic course, and considered him a wonderful student with great potential as a counselor.

    a. What do you see as possible threats to supervisor objectivity in this vignette?
    b. If you were supervising Harry, how would you want to address these possible threats in order to provide him with appropriate evaluative feedback?

4. How open are you to receiving and responding to your supervisee's formative feedback on the supervision you are providing? What is your current process for inviting and handling this type of supervisee feedback?

Table 7.2 Narrative Summary Evaluation

For her first semester of internship in her master's program in school counseling, Sally Brown was assigned to Summer Middle School. Supervision was provided in the Departmental Clinic and incorporated techniques of self-report, audio tape review, Interpersonal Process Recall (IPR), role-plays, and peer review. Sally attended 1-hour individual supervision sessions each week of the semester (15 sessions) and 2-hour group supervision sessions approximately every other week (6 sessions, 12 hours). Sally also had a 1-hour individual session with her host supervisor each week, as well as consultations on an as-needed basis.
Sally identified several learning goals for this internship experience, including recognizing client cues, developing client themes, choosing appropriate interventions for middle-school students, and developing classroom guidance presentation skills.
Sally demonstrated strong basic helping skills in both individual and group counseling sessions. She created a safe and trusting climate with all of her students. She became increasingly more adept at recognizing client cues (e.g., fidgeting with jewelry) and client themes (e.g., perfectionism). Sally was particularly adept at using confrontation, and did so with a degree of comfort notable for a first-semester intern. Her clients presented a range of issues, from sixth graders' elementary-to-middle-school-transition issues to students coping with the death of a parent. Over the course of the semester Sally conducted three psychoeducational groups on the topics of study skills for academic success, anger management and conflict resolution techniques, and orientation and 'newcomers' issues for recently enrolled immigrant children. Sally also conducted ten classroom guidance lessons on the topics of career development and career decision making skills for eighth grade students. Her guidance lesson plans were well-organized and planned and involved a variety of experiential activities. She established strong relationships with the staff at the school.
Sally came to supervision sessions well-prepared. Her case notes and session tape critiques were comprehensive and insightful. She was open to feedback from her supervisor as well as her peers, and provided constructive feedback to others during group supervision meetings. It was sometimes difficult for her to hear positive feedback.
Sally is her own most severe critic as she sets an extremely high standard for herself. Learning to accept her professional development as ongoing rather than as a finished product may be a worthwhile goal. Suggested learning goals for next semester include continued work on classroom management during guidance lessons, broadening conceptualizations of her student clients to include family influences, and use of cognitive behavioral interventions. In addition, she is encouraged to become involved in parent and teacher consultations.

In summary, Sally Brown had a full and productive first-semester internship experience as a school counselor. She is clearly on her way to becoming a school counselor who will make a strong contribution to her students and her school.

Betsy Green, PhD, Supervisor	Date
Sally Brown, Master's level Intern	Date

Chapter 8

Technology in Supervision

From typing up the documents used in each supervision session, to taping counseling sessions for use in supervision, even the simplest of supervisory relationships utilizes some form of technology. Audio- and videotaping for supervision purposes is a widely accepted form of technological intervention, but must still be further researched for most efficient and effective use (Pelling & Renard, 1999). Certainly, equipment used to play back these audio and videotapes would be included in a list of support technology. Additionally, with the current prevalence and affordability of PC cameras, it is becoming easier to record a counseling session in a digitized format, which could then be transferred to CD-ROM and played back via the supervisor's desktop computer. Live supervision has traditionally implemented technology through "bug-in-the-ear" techniques, where the supervisor uses an electronic transmitter to communicate with the counselor from behind a two-way mirror. In the past 10 years, however, available technology has grown exponentially, and keeping up with these changes is a challenge within the professions of counseling and clinical supervision.

Once you have achieved some basic level of comfort as a supervisor, you will probably want to incorporate more advanced technologies into your work. You rose to the challenge of learning about supervision models and interventions so that you might provide the best possible learning experience for your supervisees. Taking on the additional challenge of training in constantly updated supervision technology is yet another way to insure that you best serve your supervisees. As we continue to supervise novice counselors and counselors-in-training, we most likely will find that our supervisees request our utilization of the technology that will keep them on the cutting edge as counselors.

Some prevalent computer-based interventions include live supervision "bug-in-the-eye," e-mail, chat rooms and instant messaging, and cybersupervision (Watson, 2003). These different interventions vary widely in the complexity of technology required. For example, most people in today's society are familiar with the use of e-mail, and would be quite comfortable utilizing this type of technology during supervision. At the opposite end of the spectrum, the use of

DOI: 10.4324/9781003251583-8

videoconferencing for cybersupervision can involve purchasing and installing additional hardware and software for your computer, learning to problem solve when technical difficulties inevitably arise, and weathering the learning curve required for the use of this new technology.

If you are a university supervisor, you may well have access to more of the latest technology hardware and software than someone who supervises within an agency or is in private supervision practice. One example of a university-supported program is a web-based electronic portfolio used to aid in the assessment of development for school counselors-in-training (Barnes, Clark, & Thull, 2003). Another possible example might be the potential to use live supervision approaches in the university's training laboratory.

Live Supervision Technology

During our time as university supervisees, then supervisors, we have seen dramatic advances in the technology used in live supervision. In the early days, the cutting edge involved observing the supervisee's counseling session through a two-way mirror (using headphones to hear what was being said in the session), then knocking on the door to call the counselor outside when you wanted to make a suggestion for immediate implementation. Then came the use of certain "bug-in-the-ear" techniques involving ever more efficient microphones and transmitters for both the supervisee and supervisor. In this instance, the supervisor was able to observe the counseling session from another room, and also speak directly to the supervisee through a tiny receiver hidden in the supervisee's ear. The client need not even know that the supervisor is making suggestions to the supervisee at any particular point, thus making this a less intrusive form of live supervision. This method does require added concentration on the part of the supervisee, as she must learn to listen and respond to the supervisor's suggestions without significantly interrupting the flow of the ongoing counseling session (Casey, Bloom, & Moan, 1994).

Recently, a new twist to this approach has surfaced. Instead of using a transmitter in the supervisee's ear, there is a computer monitor in the counseling room, and the supervisor uses another computer behind the mirror to type verbal cues that the counselor can read, but the client cannot see. This is what has been called the "bug-in-the-eye" approach to live supervision. Some would say this is even less intrusive than the bug-in-the-ear because the typed message could be articulated with more economy, and the counselor is less likely to lose his train of thought as a result of reading a brief message from the computer screen. There is even the option of using colors or symbols to indicate certain supervisory suggestions (e.g., a smiley face icon could indicate that the supervisor thinks the counselor should focus more on feelings at this point in the session) so that the message is relayed in the most concise manner possible.

Further, with the rising use of wireless technology, supervisors can make use of handheld devices to communicate with supervisees during sessions.

Personal Digital Assistants (PDAs) can be equipped with wireless hardware connecting throughout clinics and labs for instant messaging similar to desktop software, yet appearing less intrusive due to the smaller size. Tablet PCs may also be used in a comparable way. For example, as a supervisee conducts the session and uses the tablet PC for note taking, a supervisor may communicate directly through popup messaging. In addition, the supervisee has the advantage of sending a question to the supervisor during the counseling session.

Video Technology in Supervision

Recording counseling sessions is a requirement in many counselor-training programs. Audiotapes remain the most common type of recording for supervision, yet videotaping in laboratory settings is a regular part of training both in skills classes and other clinically oriented courses. Interestingly, technology in video recording such as analog recorders (videocassette recorders for tape recording) is giving way to digital recorders with the capability of recording to Video CD, DVD, or hard disk. This innovation will allow instant access for review without the need for slow tape searching, and provide for larger storage capacities. The digital signal from these recorders also can be sent via Local Area Network (LAN) to supervisor's offices or classrooms for training purposes. In some training settings, supervisors are monitoring sessions of their supervisees and recording some or all of the session in progress for use in supervision at a designated time.

The use of digital recorders and cameras has provided supervisors and supervision instructors with additional visual information to aid in supervision, as with interpersonal process recall (Kagan, 1980). Counseling laboratories, with some modification, can easily accommodate the newest digital, perhaps wireless, technologies.

Web-Enhanced (Online) Supervision

Given that online counseling is suffering many growing pains in its early development (Heinlen, Welfel, Richmond, & Rak, 2003), there is reason to expect any type of online supervision would go through a similar developmental process. At this point, most of the concerns about using such web-based interventions as e-mail, chat rooms, or instant messaging in counseling also would hold true for use in supervision. The major concern with any of these approaches is how to best maintain client (and in our case, supervisee) confidentiality. If you plan to use e-mail or instant messaging as a regular part of your supervision process, your supervisees should be warned to protect client confidentiality in these media just as they would in any written notes by using only client initials and giving as few descriptive details as possible.

How might you use e-mail to enhance your supervisory relationships? Aside from its obvious use for scheduling sessions and site visits, your supervisees also might write to you with any pressing questions or concerns that they might need addressed before the next time they see you in a regular supervision session. With e-mail, the expected turnaround time is 24 hours, so your supervisees should know to contact you by telephone if they have an emergency or crisis situation. Another appropriate use of e-mail might be to send forms or case notes in digital format as attachments to an e-mail message. Again, this begs the question of confidentiality, but if supervisees act responsibly it really shouldn't be any more problematic than the possibility that they might lose their case notes before they could turn them in to you for review.

Instant messaging (IM), a more real-time approach to online supervision, could be used when the supervisee needs your response right now. Unlike the telephone, however, an IM program may not be readily accessible for both parties at any given time. That is, both of you would have to be online and signed on to the same IM program at the same time, which entails access to a computer with internet capabilities. Therefore, IM interactions would probably have to be scheduled beforehand, possibly through an e-mail message. The value of the IM exchange is that your supervisory suggestions can be discussed and clarified with the supervisee before he or she acts on them. IM can also lend itself to more process-oriented discussions than can an exchange of e-mails, as the interaction is much more immediate.

Chat rooms, a form of instant messaging that allows for group interactions, could allow for a broader scope of process, as other supervisees could be involved in the discussion and give their feedback. If you are a university supervisor, you should be able to set up a chat room through the university's server, to which only your current supervisees would have access. Of course, just as with any kind of group interaction, the supervisees would need to understand that each of them is responsible for maintaining the confidentiality for the group. And, finally, some IM programs give users the option to make a voice and camera connection, which would enable you and your supervisee to hear and possibly even see each other as you have this discussion. This option, however, would require the correct operating system, hardware (microphone, speakers, camera), and software be available to both parties.

It should be noted that there is some controversy within the profession about whether successful supervision could ever be entirely web-based. There is some evidence that multicultural group supervision, for example, is more effective when conducted face to face than through an entirely web-based experience (Gainor & Constantine, 2002). Because of our strong emphasis on the importance of the supervisory relationship, we believe that there should always (if at all possible) be some form of face-to-face contact with our supervisees. At the least, it is important to have met with the supervisee to establish the beginnings of the relationship, as well as learn the structure of the online supervisory experience. Ideally, the technologies discussed in this section would be used as adjuncts to the face-to-face supervision sessions.

Cybersupervision

The idea of using videoconferencing technology to conduct individual and group supervision sessions between people separated by long distances is still in its infancy. There is a need for further development and availability of this type of long-distance supervision, as evidenced by the lack of adequate supervision in the more rural and sparsely populated states such as Montana and the Dakotas. With the rise in the numbers of international students admitted to our counselor education training programs, there may well be an increase in internships in distant countries, another excellent reason to use videoconferencing supervision (Crutchfield & Bersatti, 2001).

At this point, a great deal of preparation must take place before a supervisor could meet with even a single supervisee through videoconferencing. Nonetheless, as computers, PC cameras, and other incidental hardware become ever more affordable, the once great issue of inaccessibility continues to lessen. Having had some experience in conducting long-distance videoconferencing supervision, we would like to describe one way to set this up and make it work. Included are anecdotes regarding our own learning curves with the technology, as well as our concerns about using this approach.

Although there are numerous and varied software packages available for use in videoconferencing, currently the simplest and most readily available is still Netmeeting. If you have either Windows®ME or Windows®XP operating system on your personal computer, then you already have access to the Netmeeting software. If your computer operates under an earlier system (Windows®98 or earlier), you may still go online and download this software for free. Assuming that your computer operates under Windows®ME, the following describes the process for locating Netmeeting on your computer. Using your mouse, left click on the Start button located on the tool bar, in the lower left-hand corner of your desktop screen. Moving up this pop-up menu, left click on *Programs*, then, moving your cursor over the arrow out to the right of the word, bring up the pop-up menu and left click on *Accessories*. Following these same instructions, find *Communications* on the next pop-up menu, then you will find *Netmeeting* on the menu that pops up from *Communications*. If you plan to use this software often, it would be a good idea to create a shortcut that places this Netmeeting icon on your desktop, making it more readily accessible for further use.

Once you have familiarized yourself with Netmeeting, you will need to check the audio and video settings to be sure that your PC camera is working with the software. If you do not already own a PC camera, there are many types available at very affordable prices. The newer cameras come with a built-in microphone, but if you are using an older PC camera, you will probably need to have a separate microphone or headset. In our experience, the initial difficulties of navigating the set-up of the hardware, then helping each other understand the capabilities and functions of the software, although often frustrating, can also provide a bonding experience between supervisor and supervisee, thus strengthening the supervisory relationship. It helps, however, if you are able to first meet with the supervisee at least once face to face, in order to establish the initial relationship and brainstorm possible technical issues.

The Netmeeting software allows the two individuals to see and hear each other, but there are other features that you might also want to utilize in supervision. The Chat feature is quite helpful if one of you has audio problems, as you can type messages back and forth, similar to the IM programs discussed earlier. Netmeeting also allows you to transfer files, which might mean the supervisee could send you his or her case notes or other written documents, possibly even send you sound or video files as a means of sharing a recorded or taped counseling session.

The success of any videoconferencing supervision session is dependent in part upon the technical knowledge and comfort level of both the supervisor and the supervisee. Because the supervisor is the facilitator for the interaction, the onus is on you to be able to assist the supervisee in developing his or her knowledge and comfort with the technology. When the supervisee is in another country, at times the online connection might not be a strong one, and this might interfere with the interaction as well. We have had to connect by telephone in order to reschedule a videoconference session, simply because a major thunderstorm damaged the supervisee's connection.

Although it is true that there are many technical things that could go wrong with a videoconferencing supervision session, once you and your long-distance supervisee have worked through the glitches, you may find that meeting in this way is not all that different from meeting face to face. In fact, because you are looking at a video screen, you are more likely to remain intensely focused on the supervisee, and vice versa. In our experience, the level of sharing and growth experienced by the long-distance supervisee has been as good as or better than that of the supervisee who regularly met with us in person.

Technology in Supervision Training

We have discussed numerous ways that technology can enhance the clinical supervision experience. Now we would like to briefly explore some possible uses of technology in the training of clinical supervisors. Although there are still limited options available, basic clinical supervision training can be provided through interactive CDs and accompanying manuals, allowing individuals to work at their own pace to learn theories and techniques of supervision via personal computer (Baltimore & Crutchfield, 2003). This type of training package could be used to supplement other resources in a classroom or workshop setting, or purchased individually and utilized in the professional's own time and space. At the university level, clinical supervision training for site supervisors using a Web site with streaming video and interactive techniques helps meet CACREP requirements and serves site supervisors at a distance

(Getz & Schnuman-Crook, 2002). More recently, Manzanares et al. (2004) found that site supervisors responded quite positively to their Supervisor CD-ROM, developed as a training tool to provide education and support to site supervisors. We anticipate that a number of other online and CD-ROM training programs will be developed over the next few years.

Discussion Questions

1. What types of technology are you currently using in your supervision work? How do they enhance your work? Detract from your work?
2. What would be the advantages in using Netmeeting in your supervision? What would be the disadvantages?
3. What other ethical concerns need to be considered regarding the use of technology in supervision?

Appendix A

Standards for Counseling Supervisors

SUPERVISION INTEREST NETWORK, ASSOCIATION FOR COUNSELOR EDUCATION AND SUPERVISION

The Standards for Counseling Supervisors consist of 11 core areas of knowledge, competencies, and personal traits that characterize effective supervisors.

Standards for Counseling Supervisors

(As Adopted by the AACD Governing Council, July 13–16, 1989)

The Standards include a description of eleven core areas of personal traits, knowledge and competencies that are characteristic of effective supervisors. The level of preparation and experience of the counselor and client variables will influence the relative emphasis of each competence in practice.

These core areas and their related competencies have been judged to have face validity as determined by supervisor practitioners, based on both select and widespread peer review.

1. Professional counseling supervisors are *effective counselors* whose knowledge and competencies have been acquired through training, education, and supervised employment experience.
   The counseling supervisor:

   1.1 Demonstrates knowledge of various counseling theories, systems, and their related methods;
   1.2 Demonstrates knowledge of his/her personal philosophical, theoretical and methodological approach to counseling;
   1.3 Demonstrates knowledge of his/her assumptions about human behavior; and
   1.4 Demonstrates skill in the application of counseling theory and methods (individual, group, or marital and family and specialized areas such as substance abuse, career-life rehabilitation) that are appropriate for the supervisory setting.

2. Professional counseling supervisors demonstrate *personal traits and characteristics* that are consistent with the role.
   The counseling supervisor:
   - 2.1 Is committed to updating his/her own counseling and supervisory skills;
   - 2.2 Is sensitive to individual differences;
   - 2.3 Recognizes his/her own limits through self-evaluation and feedback from others;
   - 2.4 Is encouraging, optimistic and motivational;
   - 2.5 Possesses a sense of humor;
   - 2.6 Is comfortable with the authority inherent in the role of supervisor;
   - 2.7 Demonstrates a commitment to the role of supervisor;
   - 2.8 Can identify his/her own strengths and weaknesses as a supervisor; and
   - 2.9 Can describe his/her own pattern in interpersonal relationships.
3. Professional counseling supervisors are knowledgeable regarding *ethical, legal and regulatory* aspects of the profession, and are skilled in applying this knowledge.
   The counseling supervisor:
   - 3.1 Communicates to the counselor a knowledge of professional codes of ethics (e.g., AACD, APA);
   - 3.2 Demonstrates and enforces ethical and professional standards;
   - 3.3 Communicates to the counselor an understanding of legal and regulatory documents and their impact on the profession (e.g., certification, licensure, duty to warn, parents' rights to children's records, third-party payments, etc.);
   - 3.4 Provides current information regarding professional standards (NCC, CCMHC, CRC, CCC, licensure, certification, etc.);
   - 3.5 Can communicate a knowledge of counselor rights and appeal procedures specific to the work setting; and
   - 3.6 Communicates to the counselor a knowledge of ethical considerations that pertain to the supervisory process, including dual relationships, due process evaluation, informed consent, confidentiality, and vicarious liability.
4. Professional counseling supervisors demonstrate conceptual knowledge of the *personal and professional nature of the supervisor relationship* and are skilled in applying this knowledge.
   The counseling supervisor:
   - 4.1 Demonstrates knowledge of individual differences with respect to gender, race, ethnicity, culture and age and understands the importance of these characteristics in supervisory relationships;
   - 4.2 Is sensitive to the counselor's personal and professional needs;
   - 4.3 Expects counselors to own the consequences of their actions;

4.4 Is sensitive to the evaluative nature of supervision and effectively responds to the counselor's anxiety relative to performance evaluation;
4.5 Conducts self-evaluations, as appropriate, as a means of modeling professional growth;
4.6 Provides facilitative conditions (empathy, concreteness, respect, congruence, genuineness, and immediacy);
4.7 Establishes a mutually trusting relationship with the counselor;
4.8 Provides an appropriate balance of challenge and support; and
4.9 Elicits counselor thoughts and feelings during counseling or consultation session, and responds in a manner that enhances the supervision process.

5. Professional counseling supervisors demonstrate conceptual knowledge of *supervision methods and techniques*, and are skilled in using this knowledge to promote counselor development.
The counseling supervisor:

5.1 States the purposes of supervision and explains the procedures to be used;
5.2 Negotiates mutual decisions regarding the needed direction of learning experiences for the counselor;
5.3 Engages in appropriate supervisory interventions, including role-play, role-reversal, live supervision, modeling, interpersonal process recall, micro-training, suggestions and advice, reviewing audio and video tapes, etc.;
5.4 Can perform the supervisor's functions in the role of teacher, counselor, or consultant as appropriate;
5.5 Elicits new alternatives from counselors for identifying solutions, techniques, responses to clients;
5.6 Integrates knowledge of supervision with his/her style of interpersonal relations;
5.7 Clarifies his/her role in supervision;
5.8 Uses media aids (print material, electronic recording) to enhance learning; and
5.9 Interacts with the counselor in a manner that facilitates the counselor's self-exploration and problem solving.

6. Professional counseling supervisors demonstrate conceptual knowledge of the *counselor developmental process* and are skilled in applying this knowledge.
The counseling supervisor:

6.1 Understands the developmental nature of supervision;
6.2 Demonstrates knowledge of various theoretical models of supervision;
6.3 Understands the counselor's roles and functions in particular work settings;
6.4 Understands the supervisor's roles and functions in particular work settings;

6.5 Can identify the learning needs of the counselor;
6.6 Adjusts conference content based on the counselor's personal traits, conceptual development, training, and experience; and
6.7 Uses supervisory methods appropriate to the counselor's level of conceptual development, training and experience.

7. Professional counseling supervisors demonstrate knowledge and competency in *case conceptualization and management.*
The counseling supervisor:

7.1 Recognizes that a primary goal of supervision is helping the client of the counselor;
7.2 Understands the roles of other professionals (e.g., psychologists, physicians, social workers) and assists with the referral process, when appropriate;
7.3 Elicits counselor perceptions of counseling dynamics;
7.4 Assists the counselor in selecting and executing data collection procedures;
7.5 Assists the counselor in analyzing and interpreting data objectively;
7.6 Assists the counselor in planning effective client goals and objectives;
7.7 Assists the counselor in using observation and assessment in preparation of client goals and objectives;
7.8 Assists the counselor in synthesizing client psychological and behavioral characteristics into an integrated conceptualization;
7.9 Assists the counselor in assigning priorities to counseling goals and objectives;
7.10 Assists the counselor in providing rationale for counseling procedures; and
7.11 Assists the counselor in adjusting steps in the progression toward a goal based on ongoing assessment and evaluation.

8. Professional counseling supervisors demonstrate knowledge and competency in client *assessment and evaluation.*
The counseling supervisor:

8.1 Monitors the use of tests and test interpretations;
8.2 Assists the counselor in providing rationale for assessment procedures;
8.3 Assists the counselor in communication assessment procedures and rationales;
8.4 Assists the counselor in the description, measurement, and documentation of client and counselor change; and
8.5 Assists the counselor in integrating findings and observations to make appropriate recommendations.

9. Professional counseling supervisors demonstrate knowledge and competency in *oral and written reporting and recording.*
The counseling supervisor:

9.1 Understands the meaning of accountability and the supervisor's responsibility in promoting it;

9.2 Assists the counselor in effectively documenting supervisory and counseling-related interactions;
9.3 Assists the counselor in establishing and following policies and procedures to protect the confidentiality of client and supervisory records;
9.4 Assists the counselor in identifying appropriate information to be included in a verbal or written report;
9.5 Assists the counselor in presenting information in a logical, concise, and sequential manner; and
9.6 Assists the counselor in adapting verbal and written reports to the work environment and communication situation.

10. Professional counseling supervisors demonstrate knowledge and competency in the *evaluation of counseling performance*.
The counseling supervisor:

10.1 Can interact with the counselor from the perspective of evaluator;
10.2 Can identify the counselor's professional and personal strengths, as well as weaknesses;
10.3 Provides specific feedback about such performance as conceptualization, use of methods and techniques, relationship skills, and assessment;
10.4 Determines the extent to which the counselor has developed and applied his/her own personal theory of counseling;
10.5 Develops evaluation procedures and instruments to determine program and counselor goal attainment;
10.6 Assists the counselor in the description and measurement of his/ her progress and achievement; and
10.7 Can evaluate counseling skills for purposes of grade assignment, completion of internship requirements, professional advancement, and so on.

11. Professional counseling supervisors are knowledgeable regarding *research in counseling and counselor supervision* and consistently incorporate this knowledge into the supervision process.
The counseling supervisor:

11.1 Facilitates and monitors research to determine the effectiveness of programs, services and techniques;
11.2 Reads, interprets, and applies counseling and supervisory research;
11.3 Can formulate counseling or supervisory research questions;
11.4 Reports results of counseling or supervisory research and disseminates as appropriate (e.g., inservice, conferences, publications); and
11.5 Facilitates an integration of research findings in individual case management.

The Education and Training of Supervisors

Counseling supervision is a distinct field of preparation and practice. Knowledge and competencies necessary for effective performance are acquired through a sequence of training and experience which ordinarily includes the following:

1. Graduate training in counseling;
2. Successful supervised employment as a professional counselor;
3. Credentialing in one or more of the following areas: certification by a state department of education, licensure by a state as a professional counselor, and certification as a National Certified Counselor, Certified Clinical Mental Health Counselor, Certified Rehabilitation Counselor, or Certified Career Counselor;
4. Graduate training in counseling supervision including didactic courses, seminars, laboratory courses, and supervision practica;
5. Continuing educational experiences specific to supervision theory and practice (e.g., conferences, workshops, self-study); and
6. Research activities related to supervision theory and practice.

The supervisor's primary functions are to teach the inexperienced and to foster their professional development, to serve as consultants to experienced counselors, and to assist at all levels in the provision of effective counseling services. These responsibilities require personal and professional maturity accompanied by a broad perspective on counseling that is gained by extensive, supervised counseling experience. Therefore, training for supervision generally occurs during advanced graduate study or continuing professional development. This is not to say, however, that supervisor training in the preservice stage is without merit. The presentation of basic methods and procedures may enhance students' performance as counselors, enrich their participation in the supervision process, and provide a framework for later study.

Reprinted from Dye, H. A., & Borders, L. D. (1990). Counseling supervisors: Standards for preparation and practice. *Journal of Counseling and Development*, 69, 27–32.

Appendix B

Curriculum Guide for Training Counseling Supervisors

Core Content Area: Models of Supervision

	Learning Objectives		
Major Topics	*Self-Awareness*	*Theoretical and Conceptual Knowledge*	*Skills and Techniques*
1. Elements of a model 1.1 roles of supervisor and supervisee 1.2 goals and focus of supervision 1.3 techniques for supervisee growth and change 2. Conceptual models 2.1 developmental models 2.2 theory-based models 2.3 educational ("clinical") models	1. States own beliefs and assumptions about supervision 2. Describes a personal model of supervision	1. Describes the elements of given models of supervision. (The extent of this will vary with level of training.) 2. Compares and contrasts models of supervision in terms of: 2.1 roles 2.2 goals 2.3 techniques for change 2.4 appropriateness for specific supervisees and seetings. 3. Describes research on specific models.	1. Demonstrates consistent use of a model of supervision by: 1.1 assessing a supervision session in terms of a cohesive model. 1.2 selecting interventions that are congruent with the model being used. 1.3 identifying desired outcomes based on the model. 1.4 evaluating effectiveness based on the model.

Core Content Area: Counselor Development

	Learning Objectives		
Major Topics	*Self-Awareness*	*Theoretical and Conceptual Knowledge*	*Skills and Techniques*
1. Stages of development 2. Characteristics of stages 3. Critical transition points 4. Educational environment or climate for each stage	1. Recognizes own stages of development (past and present). 2. Pursues (is open to) experiences that foster further development. 3. Demonstrates comfort with creating anxiety in supervisees. 4. Describes own feedback style. 5. Describes own learning style. 6. Describes own theory of learning (i.e., beliefs, and assumptions about how growth and change occur).	1. Describes theoretical assumptions of counselor development. 2. Relates general developmental theories (e.g., conceptual, ego) to models of counselor development. 3. Compares and contrasts several models of counselor development. 4. Differentiates between developmental level and training or experience level. 5. Describes the sequential, ongoing nature of counselor development. 6. Describes supervisory relationship dynamics at each developmental stage. 7. Describes the dynamics of an educational/learning environment (i.e., assimilation and accommodation, challenge and support). 8. Identifies interventions that create change and foster development at a particular stage. 9. Describes research on counselor development and developmental models of supervision.	1. Assesses developmental stage of supervisee, including: 1.1 general developmental (e.g., conceptual ego) levels 1.2 skill level 1.3 experience level 1.4 supervisory issues (e.g., autonomy professional identity, self-awareness). 2. Assesses learning needs of supervisee relevant to developmental level. 3. Uses interventions appropriate to counselor's developmental stage. 4. Formulates and demonstrates use of challenging interventions that create or enable change (e.g., confrontation, reframing, catalytic intervention, information giving). 5. Formulates and demonstrates use of supportive interventions (e.g., summarizing, relabeling, empathy, validation, confirmation, reinforcement). 6. Monitors interventions to create appropriate balance of challenge and support.

Core Content Area: Supervision Methods and Techniques

Major Topics	*Learning Objectives*		
	Self-Awareness	*Theoretical and Conceptual Knowledge*	*Skills and Techniques*
1. Learning needs of supervisees 1.1 assessment 1.2 goal setting 2. Interventions to foster counselor progress.	1. States own learning style and patterns. 2. States preferences and biases relative to assessment procedures. 3. States own skill and knowledge deficits relative to assessment procedures. 4. States own personal dynamics and how those interact with various assessment procedures. 5. States own preferences and biases relative to intervention methods with regard to factors such as influence, control, and support. 6. States own skill and knowledge deficits relative to intervention methods. 7. States own personal dynamics and how these interact with various supervision methods.	1. Describes the role of assessment in establishing goals and choosing supervision procedures. 2. Compares and contrasts a variety of methods of *assessment*, including: 2.1 self-report 2.2 audiotape review 2.3 videotape review 2.4 live observation. 3. States rationale for choice of assessment method. 4. Compares and contrasts various *interventions*, including: 4.1 self-reports 4.2 audiotape review 4.3 videotape review 4.4 live observation 4.5 live supervision 4.6 cocounseling.	1. Bases assessment on counselor's training, experience, and individual traits. 2. Employs a variety of assessment methods. 3. Chooses assessment method that is appropriate to counselor, setting, etc. 4. Elicits counselor participation in establishing learning objectives. 5. Manages resistance to assessment and goal setting. 6. Demonstrates use of a variety of intervention skills, including: 6.1 active listening 6.2 clarification of statements 6.3 role clarifying 6.4 giving feedback 6.5 reinforcing 6.6 confronting.

5. Compares and contrasts various intervention *formats,* including: 5.1 individual supervision 5.2 group supervision 5.3 peer supervision 5.4 team supervision. 6. States rationale for choosing particular intervention in terms of learning theory, appropriateness to counselor, client, setting, etc. 7. Describes relationship of preferred interventions to model of supervision, roles of supervisor, supervisory relationship, goals of supervision, etc. 8. Describes conceptual literature on supervision methods (i.e., models). 9. Describes research on specific interventions.	7. Demonstrates use of a variety of supervision techniques, including: 7.1 modeling 7.2 role-playing 7.3 role reversal 7.4 Interpersonal Process Recall 7.5 microtraining 7.6 behavior shaping 7.7 live observation 7.8 live supervision. 8. Applies methods in both individual and group supervision contexts. 9. Relates feedback to supervisee's learning goals. 10. Acts in teacher, counselor, or consultant roles as needed. 11. Chooses and uses interventions that provide a balance of challenge and support. 12. Fosters counselor self-exploration, self-critiquing, and problem solving.

(Continued)

Core Content Area: Supervisory Relationship

Major Topics	Learning Objectives: Self-Awareness	Learning Objectives: Theoretical and Conceptual Knowledge	Learning Objectives: Skills and Techniques
1. Individual differences 1.1 demographics (e.g., crosscultural, gender, age, ethnicity, minority, lifestyle and disability) 1.2 personality traits (e.g., learning style, motivational style, etc.) 1.3 professional variables (e.g., experience, theoretical counseling orientation, etc.) 2. Process variables 2.1 stages (beginning vs. ending) 2.2 long term vs. time limited	1. Identifies own demographic, personality, and professional variables, and states how they may affect the supervision relationship. 2. Identifies own cultural and perceptual frameworks and states how they may affect the supervisory relationship. 3. Appreciates or tolerates supervisee differences. 4. States own abilities (strengths and deficits) in initiating, maintaining, and terminating the supervisory relationship. 5. States own dynamics relative to transference, power, intimacy, trust, resistance, and parallel process.	1. Describes conceptual and empirical literature on the effects of individual differences in the supervisory relationship. 2. Describes characteristics of effective supervisory relationship. 3. Describes tasks and goals of each stage of the supervisory relationship. 4. Discriminates between processes operating in long-term vs. time-limited supervision. 5. Defines each relationship dynamic and describes how it affects supervisory relationship. 6. Describes research on supervisory relationship dynamics.	1. Demonstrates respect for individual differences in supervision session. 2. Addresses (e.g., negotiates, confronts, models, circumvents) individual differences during supervision. 3. Recognizes potential conflict areas and responds appropriately. 4. Assists counselor in recognizing own individual differences influencing the supervisory relationship. 5. Develops, maintains, and terminates supervisory relationship. 6. Modifies the intensity of the relationship across time. 7. Recognizes, in given supervision session, the occurrence of relationship dynamics.

3. Relationship dynamics (e.g., resistance, power, transference, trust, intimacy, responsibility, parallel process)	6. Accepts responsibility for quality of supervisory relationship. 7. Owns own behavior and role in problematic supervisory relationship.		8. Chooses and implements appropriate strategies that enhance the quality of the supervisory relationship. 9. Demonstrates use of skills that foster a productive supervisory relationship (e.g., confrontation, immediacy, advanced empathy, self-disclosure, interpretation). 10. Assists counselor in recognizing own interaction style and its impact on the supervisory relationship.

(*Continued*)

Core Content Area: Ethical, Legal, and Professional Regulatory Issues

Major Topics	*Learning Objectives*		
	Self-Awareness	*Theoretical and Conceptual Knowledge*	*Skills and Techniques*
1. Ethical and legal issues 1.1 dual relationship 1.2 due process 1.3 informed consent 1.4 confidentiality 1.5 liability 1.5.a. vicarious liability 1.6 consultation 1.7 privileged communication 2. Regulatory issues 2.1 professional standards 2.2 credentialing 2.3 reimbursement eligibility and procedures	1. Is sensitive to own personal vulnerabilities, including needs for support and relationship. 2. Understands own motives and professional values. 3. Acknowledges and accepts the rights of supervisees and clients for due process, informed consent, confidentiality, etc. 4. States level of personal comfort in being the bearer of highly personal information. 5. Has adequate personal security to perform supervision tasks despite legal vulnerability. 6. Recognizes and admits need for outside consultation concerning ethical and legal issues. 7. Recognizes own personal issues (e.g., status needs, desires for professional advancement, reactions to institutional authority).	1. Defines each ethical and legal term in AACD code of ethics and other relevant ethical codes that are relevant to supervision. 2. Describes subtle forms of ethical and legal dilemmas in supervision that are identified in the professional literature. 3. States legal precedents as reported in the literature that affect the practice of supervision. 4. Describes research reported in the literature on ethical and legal matters as they relate to both supervisor and counseling. 5. Describes counselor's rights and relevant appeal procedures (due process).	1. Chooses and demonstrates appropriate communication skills (e.g., confrontation, immediacy, facilitation) when faced with ethical and legal dilemmas. 2. Maintains confidentiality regarding supervision and counseling sessions. 3. Obtains informed consent as appropriate (e.g., videotaping supervision sessions, informing clients regarding supervision of counselor, etc.). 4. Informs counselors of their rights and appropriate procedures for exercising them. 5. Demonstrates decision-making skills when faced with ethical and legal dilemmas. 6. Creates appropriate boundaries within professional relationships.

2.4 institutional or agency procedures	8. Possesses a sense of own professional identity that is independent of regulatory issues. 9. States how one "measures up" to professional standards.	6. States the specific areas of coverage and limits of liability insurance. 7. States instances when outside consultation is mandatory and/or advisable. 8. Defines concept of privileged communication in counseling and supervision.	7. Requests outside intervention when dual relationships occur. 8. Manages dual relationships professionally and ethically. 9. Plans and conducts supervision to safeguard due process.

Core content Area: Ethical, Legal, and Professional Regulatory Issues

Major Topics	*Learning Objectives*		
	Self-Awareness	*Theoretical and Conceptual Knowledge*	*Skills and Techniques*
	10. Describes own status regarding credentialing as a counselor supervisor. 11. Describes own status regarding reimbursement for counseling and supervision. 12. States own attitudes and values regarding credentialing and reimbursement. 13. States own ability to thrive professionally and perform ethically within a given institutional framework.	9. Describes state regulations regarding privileged communications in counseling and supervision. 10. Describes contents of appropriate official documents, including professional standards, state laws, and institutional or agency policies. 11. Describes relevant professional literature pertaining to official documents. 12. Describes current status of professional standards and their evolution (for counseling supervision). 13. Describes current status of certification and licensure laws and how they affect counselors and supervisors. 14. Describes current actions of state boards regarding interpretation of state laws related to counseling and supervision. 15. Describes reimbursement procedures and has a working knowledge of content necessary to seek reimbursement ethically (e.g., DSM-III-R). 16. Describes how institutional or agency standards and policies regarding counseling and supervision have evolved, current status of same, and how changes are instituted.	10. Monitors supervision to cover (and attend to) realities of vicarious liability. 11. Seeks outside consultation when appropriate. 12. Maneuvers within the legal system in an ethical and professional manner. 13. Organizes data and presents self in a way that maximizes ability to obtain appropriate professional credentials. 14. Appeals to organizational groups when professional rights are denied, and helps supervisees do the same. 15. Ensures that supervisees are eligible for appropriate professional credentialing, and develops professionally within a given institutional structure. 16. Provides current information regarding professional standards for counseling. 17. Operates within institutional/agency policies while maintaining ethical and legal behavior.

Core Content Area: Evaluation

	Learning Objectives		
Major Topics	*Self-Awareness*	*Theoretical and Conceptual Knowledge*	*Skills and Techniques*
1. Role of evaluation in supervision 2. Elements of evaluation 2.1 framework 2.2 criteria and expectations 2.3 supervisory procedures 2.4 methods for monitoring 2.4 feedback mechanisms 2.5 formative evaluations 2.6 summative evaluations 3. Common issues in evaluation 3.1 anxiety 3.2 power bases and issues 3.3 discrepant evaluation 3.4 evaluation games 3.5 fit and conflict with other supervisory roles 4. Evaluating the system 4.1 feedback on the evaluation system 4.2 revising and refining evaluation activities	1. States importance of evaluation activities in supervision. 2. States comfort level with evaluative role and activities in supervision. 3. Describes personal learnings from experiences in evaluation (as counselor and supervisor). 4. Identifies preferences for evaluation procedures and sources of these preferences. 5. States own level of evaluation skills. 6. Develops plan for improving evaluation skills. 7. Demonstrates openness to feedback about self and the evaluation process.	1. Describes relationship of evaluation to other elements of supervision. 2. Describes legal, programmatic, and professional impact of evaluation. 3. Describes frameworks and methods for evaluation, including: 3.1 procedures 3.2 instruments available. 4. Compares and contrasts variety of evaluation methods, including: 4.1 self-report 4.2 audiotape review 4.3 videotape review 4.4 live observation 4.5 client indices (e.g., percentage return) 4.6 peer feedback.	1. Communicates expectations, purposes, and procedures of evaluation. 2. Negotiates a supervisory contract. 3. Gives positive and negative feedback. 4. Solicits feedback on the process of supervision, program, and supervisory relationship. 5. During evaluation, attends to counselor anxiety, differences in perception, deficient performance, client welfare concerns, ethical issues, etc. 6. Explores alternatives when evaluation plan does not work. 7. Conducts midterm evaluation report. 8. Encourages counselor self-evaluation.

Core Content Area: Evaluation

Major Topics	*Learning Objectives*		
	Self-Awareness	*Theoretical and Conceptual Knowledge*	*Skills and Techniques*
		5. Describes procedures for evaluation, including guidelines for: 5.1 giving feedback 5.2 giving bad news, confronting 5.3 positive shaping, support 5.4 avoiding destructive feedback. 6. Compares and contrasts various forms of evaluation, including: 6.1 verbal 6.2 written 6.3 behavior indicator 6.4 process 6.5 formal and informal 6.6 formative and summative. 7. Describes research on evaluation (i.e., dynamics, procedures, etc.).	9. Evaluates counseling skills for the purposes of assigning grades, professional advancement, etc. 10. Conducts formal evaluation at end of supervision meeting. 11. Writes summative evaluation report of the supervisee. 12. Elicits formal and informal evaluation of self as supervisor from counselor, colleagues, etc.

Core Content Area: Executive (Administrative) Skills

	Learning Objectives		
Major Topics	*Self-Awareness*	*Theoretical and Conceptual Knowledge*	*Skills and Techniques*
1. Organization 1.1 planning 1.2 recordkeeping 1.3 reporting 1.4 collaboration 1.5 workable procedures 1.6 research and evaluation 2. The institution or agency 2.1 role clarification 2.2 supervisee rights 2.3 expectations 3. Protecting client welfare 3.1 client-counselor assignments 3.2 case management	1. Describes own leadership and organizational style and its impact on others, including strengths and limitations of own style. 2. Understands and values the purpose (s) of data collection, documentation, and recordkeeping. 3. Describes own oral and written communication style, including strengths and limitations. 4. Describes own relationships with other departments and personnel. 5. Describes own good and bad work habits (e.g., attendance, punctuality, responsiveness to telephone calls, etc.). 6. Demonstrates comfort with multiple roles and with their impact on the supervisee (e.g., supervisor and administrator, supervisor and professor).	1. Describes various leadership and organizational styles and their values and limitations. 2. Describes a variety of methods of recordkeeping and data collection. 3. Describes ethical, legal, and regulatory guidelines for recordkeeping. 4. Describes professional standards for oral and written language usage. 5. Describes accountability issues and their importance to the profession. 6. Describes roles and responsibilities of other staff members, departments, and agencies or institutions. 7. Describes institutional needs, standards, procedures, and policies. 8. Describes program evaluation theory and practices.	1. Plans an effective supervision program (e.g., logistics, schedules, calendars, efficient resource utilization, goal setting). 2. Solicits input and feedback from supervisees. 3. Assists supervisees in identifying an organization style that is effective for them and meets guidelines. 4. Assists supervisees in communicating effectively in their verbal and written reports. 5. Assists the counselor in the description, management, and documentation of client and counselor change. 6. Maintains networks for effective collaboration. 7. Assists with the referral process as needed or appropriate.

(Continued)

Core Content Area: Executive (Administrative) Skills

Major Topics	*Learning Objectives*		
	Self-Awareness	*Theoretical and Conceptual Knowledge*	*Skills and Techniques*
	7. Describes own strengths and weaknesses as an administrator. 8. States parameters of the administrator vs. supervisory roles. 9. States own expectations and standards as an administrator. 10. Recognizes that a primary goal of supervision is helping the clients of the counselor (supervisee). 11. Articulates a theoretical base for matching clients and counselors. 12. States own beliefs and blind spots regarding matching clients and counselors. 13. Demonstrates (to clients) safety issues, both physical and psychological. 14. States own beliefs about and processes for managing clients' cases.	9. Describes rationale for conducting program evaluation. 10. Describes current research findings relevant to program evaluation. 11. Describes the vocabulary, concepts, and practices for implementing various roles. 12. Describes counselor's role within the mission of the agency or institution. 13. States the agency or institution's definition of the counselor's role. 14. States agency or institution's expectations for the supervisory process. 15. States agency or institution's standards for work habits. 16. Describes institutional or agency definitions of "standard practices."	8. Develops and communicates efficient and appropriate procedures. 9. Reads, writes, and interprets standards, procedures, and policies. 10. Applies current, relevant research in organizational plans. 11. Conducts formative and summative evaluations of counselor and of the counseling program or agency, and reports findings. 12. Develops evaluation procedures and instruments to determine program and counselor goal attainment. 13. Facilitates and monitors program evaluation. 14. Reports results of program evaluation and disseminates appropriately (e.g., inservice conferences, publications).

15. States own strengths and limitations in case management.	17. States importance of establishing emergency procedures. 18. Describes emergency and crisis procedures of institution or agency. 19. Describes case management theory and practices.	15. Articulates own multiple roles clearly to the counselor. 16. Assists supervisees to differentiate between the various roles of the supervisor. 17. Assists supervisees to define their role(s) appropriately, including the parameters of the counseling role. 18. Articulates purposes of administrative vs. counseling supervisions. 19. Develops an effective plan for administrative supervision, based on expectation and goals of agency or institution and themselves. 20. Expresses standards for work habits. 21. Assists counselor's formative and summative evaluation of own changes. 22. Evaluates supervisees appropriately. 23. Ensures appropriate matches between client needs and counselor competence. 24. Intervenes in counselor-client relationship appropriately, including emergency or crisis situations.

(*Continued*)

Major Topics	*Learning Objectives*		
	Self-Awareness	*Theoretical and Conceptual Knowledge*	*Skills and Techniques*
			25. Communicates procedures to counselor in manner that respects both client and counselor. 26. Teaches the counselor case management skills. 27. Establishes and implements a system for monitoring supervisees' management of cases.

Reprinted from Borders, L.D., Bernard, J. M., Dye, H. A., Fong, M. L., Henderson, P., & Nance, D. W. (1991). Curriculum guide for training counseling supervisors: Rationale, development, and implementation. *Counselor Education and Supervision, 31*, 58–80.

Appendix C

Ethical Guidelines for Counseling Supervisors

The following *Ethical Guidelines for Counseling Supervisors* were adopted by the Association for Counselor Education and Supervision (ACES) Governing Council in March of 1993. The guidelines were written by a subcommittee of the ACES Supervision Interest Group, which comprised the following members: Gordon Hart, Chair; L. DiAnne Borders; Don Nance; and Louis Paradise. The guidelines first appeared in ACES Spectrum, Volume 53, Number 4, Summer 1993.

Preamble

The Association for Counselor Education and Supervision (ACES) is composed of people engaged in the professional preparation of counselors and people responsible for the ongoing supervision of counselors. ACES is a founding division of the American Counseling Association (ACA) and, as such, adheres to the ACA's current *Ethical Standards* (ACA, 1988) and to general codes of competence adopted throughout the mental health community.

ACES believes that counselor educators and counseling supervisors in universities and in applied counseling settings, including the range of education and mental health delivery systems, carry responsibilities unique to their job roles. Such responsibilities may include administrative supervision, clinical supervision, or both. Administrative supervision refers to those supervisory activities that increase the efficiency of the delivery of counseling services, whereas clinical supervision includes the supportive and educative activities of the supervisor designed to improve the application of counseling theory and technique directly to clients.

Counselor educators and counseling supervisors encounter situations that challenge the help given by general ethical standards of the profession at large. These situations require more specific guidelines that provide appropriate guidance in everyday practice.

The *Ethical Guidelines for Counseling Supervisors* are intended to assist professionals by helping them:

1. Observe ethical and legal protection of clients' and supervisees' rights;
2. Meet the training and professional development needs of supervisees in ways consistent with clients' welfare and programmatic requirements; and
3. Establish policies, procedures, and standards for implementing programs.

The specification of ethical guidelines enables ACES members to focus on and to clarify the ethical nature of responsibilities held in common. Such guidelines should be reviewed formally every 5 years, or more often if needed, to meet the needs of ACES members for guidance.

The *Ethical Guidelines for Counseling Supervisors* are meant to help ACES members in conducting supervision. ACES is not currently in a position to hear complaints about alleged noncompliance with these guidelines. Any complaints about the ethical behavior of any ACA member should be measured against the ACA *Ethical Standards* and a complaint lodged with ACA in accordance with their procedures for doing so.

One overriding assumption underlying this document is that supervision should be ongoing throughout a counselor's career and should not stop when a particular level of education, certification, or membership in a professional organization is attained.

Definitions of Terms

Applied Counseling Settings—Public or private organizations of counselors such as community mental health centers, hospitals, schools, and group or individual private practice settings.

Supervisees—Counselors-in-training in university programs at any level who are working with clients in applied settings as part of their university training program, and counselors who have completed their formal education and are employed in an applied counseling setting.

Supervisors—Counselors who have been designated within their university or agency to directly oversee the professional clinical work of counselors. Supervisors also may be persons who offer supervision to counselors seeking state licensure and so provide supervision outside of the administrative aegis of an applied counseling setting.

1. Client Welfare and Rights

1.01 The primary obligation of supervisors is to train counselors so that they respect the integrity and promote the welfare of their clients. Supervisors should have supervisees inform clients that they are being supervised and that observation or recordings of the session may be reviewed by the supervisor.

1.02 Supervisors who are licensed counselors and are conducting supervision to aid a supervisee to become licensed should instruct the supervisee not to communicate or in any way convey to the supervisee's clients or to other parties that the supervisee is himself or herself licensed.

1.03 Supervisors should make supervisees aware of clients' rights, including protecting clients' right to privacy and confidentiality in the counseling relationship and the information resulting from it. Clients also should be informed that their right to privacy and confidentiality will not be violated by the supervisory relationship.

1.04 Records of the counseling relationship, including interview notes, test date, correspondence, the electronic storage of these documents, and audio and videotape recordings are considered to be confidential professional information. Supervisors should see that these materials are used in counseling, research, and training and supervision of counselors with the full knowledge of the client and that permission to use these materials is granted by the applied counseling setting offering service to the client. This professional information is to be used for the full protection of the client. Written consent from the client (or legal guardian, if a minor) should be secured prior to the use of such information for instructional, supervisory, or research purposes. Policies of the applied counseling setting regarding client records also should be followed.

1.05 Supervisors shall adhere to current professional and legal guidelines when conducting research with human beings such as Section D-l of the ACA *Ethical Standards*.

1.06 Counseling supervisors are responsible for making every effort to monitor both the professional actions, and failures to take action, of their supervisees.

2. *Supervisory Role*

Inherent and integral to the role of supervisor are responsibilities for:

a. Monitoring client welfare;
b. Encouraging compliance with relevant legal, ethical, and professional standards for clinical practice;
c. Monitoring clinical performance and professional development of supervisees; and
d. Evaluating and certifying current performance and potential of supervisees for academic, screening, selection, placement, employment, and credentialing purposes.

2.01 Supervisors should have had training in supervision prior to initiating their role as supervisors.

2.02 Supervisors should pursue professional and personal continuing education activities such as advanced courses, seminars, and professional conferences on a regular and ongoing basis. These activities should include both counseling and supervision topics and skills.

2.03 Supervisors should make their supervisees aware of professional and ethical standards and legal responsibilities of the counseling profession.

2.04 Supervisors of postdegree counselors who are seeking state licensure should encourage these counselors to adhere to the standards for practice established by the state licensure board of the state in which they practice.

2.05 Procedures for contacting the supervisor, or an alternative supervisor, to assist in handling crisis situations should be established and communicated to supervisees.

2.06 Actual work samples via audio- or videotape or live observation in addition to case notes should be reviewed by the supervisor as a regular part of the ongoing supervisory process.

2.07 Supervisors of counselors should meet regularly in face-to-face sessions with their supervisees.

2.08 Supervisors should provide supervisees with ongoing feedback on their performance. This feedback should take a variety of forms, both formal and informal, and should include verbal and written evaluation. It should be formative during the supervisory experience and summative at the conclusion of the experience.

2.09 Supervisors who have multiple roles (e.g., teacher, clinical supervisor, administrative supervisor) with supervisees should minimize potential conflicts. When possible, the roles should be divided among several supervisors. When this is not possible, careful explanation should be conveyed to the supervisee as to the expectations and responsibilities associated with each supervisory role.

2.10 Supervisors should not participate in any form of sexual contact with supervisees. Supervisors should not engage in any form of social contact or interaction that would compromise the supervisor-supervisee relationship. Dual relationships with supervisees that might impair the supervisor's objectivity and professional judgment should be avoided or the supervisory relationship terminated.

2.11 Supervisors should not establish a psychotherapeutic relationship as a substitute for supervision. Personal issues should be addressed in supervision only in terms of the effect of these issues on clients and on professional functioning.

2.12 Supervisors, through ongoing supervisee assessment and evaluation, should be aware of any personal or professional limitations of supervisees that are likely to impede future professional performance. Supervisors have the responsibility of recommending remedial assistance to the supervisee and of screening from the training program, applied counseling setting, or state licensure those supervisees who are unable to provide competent professional services. These recommendations should be clearly and professionally explained in writing to the supervisees who are so evaluated.

2.13 Supervisors should not endorse a supervisee for certification, licensure, completion of an academic training program, or continued employment if the supervisor believes the supervisee is impaired in any way that would interfere with the performance of counseling duties. The presence of any such impairment should begin a process of feedback and remediation wherever possible so that the supervisee understands the nature of the impairment and has the opportunity to remedy the problem and continue with his or her professional development.

2.14 Supervisors should incorporate the principles of informed consent and participation; clarity of requirements, expectations, roles and rules; and due process and appeal into the establishment of policies and procedures of their institution, program, courses, and individual supervisory relationships. Mechanisms for due process appeal of individual supervisory actions should be established and made available to all supervisees.

3. *Program Administration Role*

3.01 Supervisors should ensure that the programs conducted and experiences provided are in keeping with current guidelines and standards of ACA and its divisions.

3.02 Supervisors should teach courses or supervise clinical work only in areas in which they are fully competent and experienced.

3.03 To achieve the highest quality of training and supervision, supervisors should be active participants in peer review and peer supervision procedures.

3.04 Supervisors should provide experiences that integrate theoretical knowledge and practical application. Supervisors also should provide opportunities in which supervisees are able to apply the knowledge they have learned and understand the rationale for the skills they have acquired. The knowledge and skills conveyed should reflect current practice, research findings, and available resources.

3.05 Professional competencies, specific courses, or required experiences expected of supervisees should be communicated to them in writing prior to admission to the training program, placement, or employment by the applied counseling setting, and, in case of continued employment, in a timely manner.

3.06 Supervisors should accept only those persons as supervisees who meet identified entry-level requirements for admission to a program of counselor training or placement in an applied counseling setting. In the case of private supervision in search of state licensure, supervisees should have completed all necessary prerequisites as determined by the state licensure board.

3.07 Supervisors should inform supervisees of the goals, policies, theoretical orientations toward counseling, training, and supervision model or approach in which the supervision is based.

3.08 Supervisees should be encouraged and assisted to define their own theoretical orientation toward counseling, to establish supervision goals for themselves, and to monitor and evaluate their progress toward meeting these goals.

3.09 Supervisors should assess supervisees' skills and experience to establish standards for competent professional behavior. Supervisors should restrict supervisees' activities to those that are commensurate with their current level of skills and experiences.

3.10 Supervisors should obtain practicum and fieldwork sites that meet minimum standards for preparing students to become effective counselors. No practicum or fieldwork setting should be approved unless it truly replicates a counseling work setting.

3.11 Practicum and fieldwork classes should be limited in size according to established professional standards to ensure that each student has ample opportunity for individual supervision and feedback. Supervisors in applied counseling settings should have a limited number of supervisees.

3.12 Supervisors in university settings should establish and communicate specific policies and procedures regarding field placement of students. The respective roles of the student counselor, the university supervisor, and the field supervisor should be clearly differentiated in areas such as evaluation, requirements, and confidentiality.

3.13 Supervisors in training programs should communicate regularly with supervisors in agencies used as practicum or fieldwork sites regarding current professional practices, expectations of students, and preferred models and modalities of supervision.

3.14 Supervisors at the university should establish clear lines of communication among themselves, the field supervisors, and the students or supervisees.

3.15 Supervisors should establish and communicate to supervisees and to field supervisors specific procedures regarding consultation, performance review, and evaluation of supervisees.

3.16 Evaluations of supervisee performance in universities and in applied counseling settings should be available to supervisees in ways consistent with the Family Rights and Privacy Act.

3.17 Forms of training that focus primarily on self-understanding and problem resolution (e.g., personal growth groups or individual counseling) should be voluntary. Those who conduct these forms of training should not serve simultaneously as supervisors of the supervisees involved in the training.

3.18 A supervisor may recommend participation in activities such as personal growth groups or personal counseling when it has been determined that a supervisee has deficits in the areas of self understanding and problem resolution that impede his or her professional functioning. The supervisor should not be the direct provider of these activities for the supervisee.

3.19 When a training program conducts a personal growth or counseling experience involving relatively intimate self-disclosure, care should be taken to eliminate or minimize potential role conflicts for faculty or agency supervisors who may conduct these experiences and who also serve as teachers, group leaders, and clinical directors.

3.20 Supervisors should use the following prioritized sequence in resolving conflicts among the needs of the client, the needs of the supervisee, and the needs of the program or agency. Insofar as the client must be protected, it should be understood that client welfare is usually subsumed in federal and state laws such that these statutes should be the first point of reference. When laws and ethical standards are not present or are unclear, the good judgment of the supervisor should be guided by the following list:

a. Relevant legal and ethical standards (e.g., duty to warn, state child abuse laws, etc.);
b. Client welfare;
c. Supervisee welfare;
d. Supervisor welfare; and
e. Program or agency service and administrative needs.

REFERENCE

American Counseling Association. (1988). Ethical standards (3rd revision). *Journal of Counseling and Development, 67,* 4–8.

References

Akamatsu, T. J. (1980). The use of role-play and simulation techniques in the training of psychotherapy. In A. K. Hess (Ed.), *Psychotherapy supervision: Theory, research and practice* (pp. 209–225). New York: Wiley.

American Counseling Association. (1988). *Ethical standards*. Alexandria, VA: Author.

Amundson, N. (1988). The use of metaphor and case drawing in case conceptualization. *Journal of Counseling and Development,* 66, 391–393.

Anderson, T. (1987). The reflecting team: Dialogue and meta-dialogue in clinical work. *Family Process, 26,* 415–428.

Baltimore, M. L., & Crutchfield, L. B. (2003). *Clinical supervisor training: An interactive CD-ROM training program for the helping professions*. Boston: Allyn & Bacon.

Baltimore, M. L., Crutchfield, L. B., Gillam, S. L., & Lee, R. W. (2001, August 3). *Ethics in supervision: Process, practice, and guidelines for the helping professions.* Workshop presented at Columbus State University, Columbus, GA.

Barnes, P. E., Clark, P., & Thull, B. (2003). Web-based digital portfolios and counselor supervision. *Journal of Technology in Counseling, 3*(1). Retrieved November 5, 2003, from http://jtc/colstate.edu/vol3_1/Barnes/Barnes.htm

Benshoff, J. M., Borders, L. D., & Daniel, R. L. (2001). *Managing liability in clinical supervision* [Instructional videotape]. Alexandria, VA: American Counseling Association.

Bernard, J. M. (1979). Supervisory training: A discrimination model. *Counselor Education and Supervision, 19,* 60–68.

Bernard, J. M. (1989). Training supervisors to examine relationship variables using IPR. *The Clinical Supervisor, 7*(1), 103–112.

Bernard, J. M. (1997). The discrimination model. In C. E. Watkins, Jr. (Ed.), *Handbook of psychotherapy supervision* (pp. 310–327). New York: Wiley.

Bernard, J. M., & Goodyear, R. K. (1992). *Fundamentals of clinical supervision.* Needham Heights, MA: Allyn & Bacon.

Bernard, J. M., & Goodyear, R. K. (1998). *Fundamentals of clinical supervision* (2nd ed.). Needham Heights, MA: Allyn & Bacon.

Bernard, J. M., & Goodyear, R. K. (2004). *Fundamentals of clinical supervision* (3rd ed.). Needham Heights, MA: Allyn & Bacon.

Blocher, D. H. (1983). Toward a cognitive developmental approach to counseling supervision. *The Counseling Psychologist, 11*(1), 27–34.

Blumberg, A. (1968). Supervisor behavior and interpersonal relations. *Educational Administration Quarterly*, *5*, 34–45.

Borders, L. D. (1989). A pragmatic agenda for developmental supervision research. *Counselor Education and Supervision*, *29*, 16–24.

Borders, L. D. (1991). A systematic approach to peer group supervision. *Journal of Counseling and Development*, *69*, 248–252.

Borders, L. D. (1992). Learning to think like a supervisor. *The Clinical Supervisor*, *10(2)*, 135–148.

Borders, L. D. (1994). The good supervisor. In L. D. Borders (Ed.), *Supervision: Exploring the effective components* (ERIC Document Reproduction Service No. EDO-CD-94–19). Greensboro, NC: ERIC/CASS.

Borders, L. D. (2001). Counseling supervision: A deliberate educational process. In D. C. Locke, J. E. Myers, & E. L. Herr (Eds.), *The handbook of counseling* (pp. 417–432). Thousand Oaks, CA: Sage.

Borders, L. D. (2004). *Anxiety and resistance: Dealing with challenges of skill and patience*. Unpublished manuscript.

Borders, L. D., & Benshoff, J. M. (1999). *Learning to think like a supervisor* [Instructional videotape]. Alexandria, VA: American Counseling Association.

Borders, L. D., Bernard, J. M., Dye, H. A., Fong, M. L., Henderson, P., & Nance, D. W. (1991). Curriculum guide for training counseling supervisors: Rationale, development, and implementation. *Counselor Education and Supervision, 31*, 58–80.

Borders, L. D., & Cashwell, C. S. (1992). Supervision regulations in counselor licensure legislation. *Counselor Education and Supervision, 31*, 208–218.

Borders, L. D., Cashwell, C. S., & Rotter, J. C. (1995). Supervision of counselor licensure applicants: A comparative study. *Counselor Education and Supervision, 35*, 54–69.

Borders, L. D., & Fong, M. L. (1994). Cognitions of supervisors-in-training: An exploratory study. *Counselor Education and Supervision, 33*, 280–293.

Borders, L. D., & Leddick, G. R. (1987). *Handbook of counseling supervision*. Alexandria, VA: Association for Counselor Education and Supervision.

Borders, L. D., & Usher, C. H. (1992). Post-degree supervision: Existing and preferred practices. *Journal of Counseling and Development, 70*, 594–599.

Bordin, E. S. (1983). A working alliance based model of supervision. *The Counseling Psychologist, 11*(1), 35–42.

Bowlby, J. (1973). *Attachment and loss: Vol. 2. Separation, anxiety, and anger*. New York: Basic Books.

Bradley, L. J., & Gould, L. J. (1994). Supervisee resistance. In L. D. Borders (Ed.), *Supervision: Exploring the effective components* (ERIC Document Reproduction Service No. EDO-CD-94–43). Greensboro, NC: ERIC/CASS.

Bradley, L. J., & Gould, L. J. (2001). Psychotherapy-based models of counselor supervision. In L. J. Bradley & N. Ladany (Eds.), *Counselor supervision: Principles, process, and practice* (pp. 147–180). Philadelphia: Brunner-Routledge.

Brown, M. T., & Landrum-Brown, J. (1995). Counselor supervision: Cross-cultural perspectives. In J. G. Ponterotto, J. M. Cacas, L. A. Suzuki, & C. M. Alexander (Eds.), *Handbook of multicultural counseling* (pp. 263–286). Thousand Oaks, CA: Sage.

Bubenzer, D. L., Mahrle, C., & West, J. D. (1987). *Live counselor supervision: Trainee acculturation and supervision intentions.* Paper presented at the annual meeting of the American Association of Counseling and Development, New Orleans, LA.

Buhrke, R. A. (1988). Lesbian-related issues in counseling supervision. *Women and Therapy, 8*, 195–206.

Buhrke, R. A. (1989). Incorporating lesbian and gay issues into counselor training: A resource guide. *Journal of Counseling and Development, 68,* 77–80.

Casey, J. A., Bloom, J. W., & Moan, E. R. (1994). Use of technology in counselor supervision. In L. D. Borders (Ed.), *Supervision: Exploring the effective components* (ERIC Document Reproduction Service No. EDO-CD-94–26). Greensboro, NC: ERIC/CASS.

Cashwell, C. S. (1994). Interpersonal process recall. In L. D. Borders (Ed.), *Supervision: Exploring the effective components* (ERIC Document Reproduction Service No. EDO-CD-94–11). Greensboro, NC: ERIC/CASS.

Christensen, T. M., & Kline, W. B. (2001). The qualitative exploration of process-sensitive peer group supervision. *Journal for Specialists in Group Work, 26,* 81–99.

Claiborn, C. D., Etringer, B. D., & Hillerbrand, E. T. (1995). Influence processes in supervision. *Counselor Education and Supervision, 35*, 43–53.

Cobia, D. C., & Boes, S. R. (2000). Professional disclosure statements and formal plans for supervision: Two strategies for minimizing the risk of ethical conflicts in post-master's supervision. *Journal of Counseling and Development, 78,* 293–296.

Constantine, M. (1997). Facilitating multicultural competency in counseling supervision: Operationalizing a practical framework. In D. B. Pope-Davis & H. L. K. Coleman (Eds.), *Multicultural counseling competencies: Assessment, education and training, and supervision* (pp. 310–324). Thousand Oaks, CA: Sage.

Cook, D. A. (1994). Racial identity in supervision. *Counselor Education and Supervision, 34*, 132–141.

Corey, G., Corey, M. S., & Callanan, P. (1998). *Issues and ethics in the helping professions* (5th ed.). Pacific Grove, CA: Brooks/Cole.

Council for Accreditation of Counseling and Related Educational Programs. (2001). *CACREP accreditation standards and procedure manual.* Alexandria, VA: Author.

Crutchfield, L. B., & Bersatti, R. (2001, October). *Long distance video supervision: A case study.* Presentation at the annual conference of Southern Association for Counselor Education and Supervision, Athens, GA.

Crutchfield, L. B., & Borders, L. D. (1997). Impact of two clinical peer supervision models on practicing school counselors. *Journal of Counseling and Development, 75,* 219–230.

Daniels, T. G., Rigazio-DiGilio, S. A., & Ivey, A. E. (1997). Microcounseling: A training and supervision paradigm in the helping professions. In C. E. Watkins, Jr. (Ed.), *Handbook of psychotherapy supervision* (pp. 277–295). New York: Wiley.

Dean, J. E. (2001). Sandtray consultation: A method of supervision applied to couple's therapy. *The Arts in Psychotherapy, 28,* 175–180.

DeLucia-Waack, J. L. (1999). Supervision for counselors working with eating disorder groups: Countertransference issues related to body image, food, and weight. *Journal of Counseling and Development, 77*, 379–388.

Dewald, P. A. (1987). *Learning process in psychoanalytic supervision: Complexities and challenges, a case illustration.* Madison, CT: International Universities Press.

Disney, M. J., & Stephens, A. M. (1994). *Legal issues in clinical supervision* [ACA legal series, Vol. 10]. Alexandria, VA: American Counseling Association.

Dixon, D. N., & Claiborn, C. D. (1987). A social influence approach to counselor supervision. In J. E. Maddux, C. D. Stoltenberg, & R. Rosenwein (Eds.), *Social processes in clinical and counseling psychology* (pp. 83–93). New York: Springer-Verlag.

Doehrman, M. J. (1976). Parallel processes in supervision and psychotherapy. *Bulletin of the Menninger Clinic, 40,* 1–104.

Duan, C., & Roehlke, H. (2001). A descriptive "snapshot" of cross-racial supervision in university counseling center internships. *Journal of Multicultural Counseling and Development, 29*, 131–146.

Dye, A. (1994). The supervisory relationship. In L. D. Borders (Ed.), *Supervision: Exploring the effective components* (ERIC Document Reproduction Service No. EDO-CD-94–42). Greensboro, NC: ERIC/CASS.

Dye, H. A., & Borders, L. D. (1990). Counseling supervisors: Standards for preparation and practice. *Journal of Counseling and Development, 69*, 27–32.

Efstation, J. F., Patton, M. J., & Kardash, C. M. (1990). Measuring the working alliance in counselor supervision. *Journal of Counseling Psychology, 37*, 322–329.

Ekstein, R., & Wallerstein, R. S. (1972). *The teaching and learning of psychotherapy* (2nd ed.). New York: International Universities Press.

Elizur, J. (1990). "Stuckness" in live supervision: Expanding the therapist's *style. Journal of Family Therapy, 12*, 267–280.

Ellis, M. V., & Deli, D. M. (1986). Dimensionality of supervisor roles: Supervisors' perceptions of supervision. *Journal of Counseling Psychology, 33*, 282–291.

Ellis, M. V., & Ladany, N. (1997). Inferences concerning supervisees and clients in clinical supervision: An integrative review. In C. E. Watkins, Jr. (Ed.), *Handbook of psychotherapy supervision* (pp. 447–507). New York: Wiley.

Fall, M., & Sutton, J. M., Jr. (2004). *Clinical supervision: A handbook for practitioners.* Boston: Pearson/Allyn & Bacon.

Falvey, J. E., Caldwell, C. F., & Cohen, C. R. (2002). *Documentation in supervision: The focused risk management supervision system FoRMSS.* Pacific Grove, CA: Brooks/Cole.

Fong, M. L. (1994). Multicultural issues in supervision. In L. D. Borders (Ed.), *Supervision: Exploring the effective components* (ERIC Document Reproduction Service No. EDO-CD-94–15). Greensboro, NC: ERIC/CASS.

Fong, M. L., & Lease, S. H. (1997). Cross-cultural supervision: Issues for the white supervisor. In D. B. Pope-Davis & H. L. K. Coleman (Eds.), *Multicultural counseling competencies: Assessment, education and training, and supervision* (pp. 387–405). Thousand Oaks, CA: Sage.

Forsyth, D. R., & Ivey, A. E. (1980). Micro training: An approach to differential supervision. In A. K. Hess (Ed.), *Psychotherapy supervision: Theory, research and practice* (pp. 242–261). New York: Wiley.

Friedlander, M. L., Keller, K. E., Peca-Baker, T. A., & Olk, M. E. (1986). Effects of role conflict on counselor trainees' self-statements, anxiety level, and performance. *Journal of Counseling Psychology, 33*, 73–77.

Friedlander, M. L., & Ward, L. G. (1984). Development and validation of the Supervisory Styles Inventory. *Journal of Counseling Psychology, 31*, 541–557.

Friedman, R. (1983). Aspects of the parallel process and counter-tranference issues in student supervision. *School Social Work Journal, 8*(1), 3–15.

Gainor, K. A., & Constantine, M. G. (2002). Multicultural groups of supervision: A comparison of in-person versus web-based formats. *Professional School Counseling, 6*, 104–111.

Gatmon, D., Jackson, D., Koshkarian, L., Martos-Perry, N., Molina, A., Patel, N., & Rodolfa, E. (2001). Exploring ethnic, gender, and sexual orientation variables in supervision: Do they matter? *Journal of Multicultural Counseling and Development, 29*, 102–113.

Getz, H. G., & Schnuman-Crook, A. (2002). Utilization of online training for on-site clinical supervisors: One university's approach. *Journal of Technology in Counseling, 2*(1). Retrieved November 5, 2003, from http.//jtc.colstate.edu/vol2_l/Supervisors.htm

Goldberg, D. A. (1983). Resistance to the use of video in individual psychotherapy training. *American Journal of Psychiatry, 140*, 1172–1176.

Goldberg, D. A. (1985). Process notes, audio, and videotape: Modes of presentation in psychotherapy training. *The Clinical Supervisor, 3*(3), 3–14.

Goodyear, R. K., & Nelson, M. L. (1997). The major formats of psychotherapy supervision. In C. E. Watkins, Jr. (Ed.), *Handbook of psychotherapy supervision* (pp. 328–344). New York: Wiley.

Gray, L. A., Ladany, N., Walker, J. A., & Ancis, J. R. (2001). Psychotherapy trainees' experience of counterproductive events in supervision. *Journal of Counseling Psychology, 48*, 371–383.

Greenberg, L. (1980). Training counsellors in Gestalt methods. *Canadian Counsellor, 15*, 174–180.

Hackney, H., & Goodyear, R. K. (1984). Carl Rogers' client-centered approach to supervision. In R. F. Levant & J. M. Shlein (Eds.), *Client-centered therapy and the person-centered approach: New directions in theory, research, and practice* (pp. 278–296). New York: Praeger.

Hart, G., Borders, L. D., Nance, D., & Paradise, L. (1995). Ethical guidelines for counseling supervisors. *Counselor Education and Supervision, 34*, 270–276.

Harvey, O. J., Hunt, D. E., & Schroeder, H. (1961). *Conceptual systems and personality organization.* New York: Wiley.

Hawthorne, L. (1975). Games supervisors play. *Social Work, 20*, 179–183.

Hays, D. G., & Chang, C. Y. (2003). White privilege, oppression, and racial identity development: Implications for supervision. *Counselor Education and Supervision, 43*, 134–145.

Heinlen, K. T., Welfel, E. R., Richmond, E. N., & Rak, C. F. (2003). The scope of WebCounseling: A survey of services and compliance with NBCC *Standards for the Ethical Practice of WebCounseling. Journal of Counseling and Development, 81*, 61–69.

Hillerbrand, E. (1989). Cognitive differences between experts and novices: Implications for group supervision. *Journal of Counseling and Development, 67*, 293–296.

Hird, J. S., Cavalieri, C. E., Dulko, J. P., Felice, A. A. D., & Ho, T. A. (2001). Visions and realities: Supervisee perspectives of multicultural supervision. *Journal of Multicultural Counseling and Development, 29*, 114–130.

Hoffman, R. M., Borders, L. D., & Hattie, J. A. (2000). Reconceptualizing femininity and masculinity: From gender roles to gender self-confidence. *Journal of Social Behavior and Personality, 15*, 475–503.

Holloway, E. L. (1995). *Clinical supervision: A systems approach.* Thousand Oaks, CA: Sage.

Holloway, E. L. (1997). Structures for the analysis and teaching of supervision. In C. E. Watkins, Jr. (Ed.), *Handbook of psychotherapy supervision* (pp. 249–276). New York: Wiley.

Holloway, E. L., & Wampold, B. E. (1983). Patterns of verbal behavior and judgments of satisfaction in the supervision interview. *Journal of Counseling Psychology, 30*, 227–234.

Hosford, R. E., & Barmann, B. (1983). A social learning approach to counselor supervision. *The Counseling Psychologist, 11*(1), 51–58.

Ishiyama, F. (1988). A model of visual case processing using metaphor and drawings. *Counselor Education and Supervision, 28*, 153–161.

Ivey, A. E. (1994). *Intentional interviewing and counseling: Facilitating client development in a multicultural society.* Pacific Grove, CA: Brooks/Cole.

Kadushin, A. (1968). Games people play in supervision. *Social Work, 13*, 23–32.

Kagan (Klein), H., & Kagan, N. I. (1997). Interpersonal process recall: Influencing human interaction. In C. E. Watkins, Jr. (Ed.), *Handbook of psychotherapy supervision* (pp. 296–309). New York: Wiley.

Kagan, N. (1975). *Interpersonal process recall: A method of influencing human interaction.* East Lansing: MI: Michigan State University.

Kagan, N. (1980). Influencing human interaction—Eighteen years with IPR. In A. K. Hess (Ed.), *Psychotherapy supervision: Theory, research and practice* (pp. 262–283). New York: Wiley.

Klitzke, M. J., & Lombardo, T. W. (1991). A "bug-in-the-eye" can be better than a "bug-in-the-ear": A teleprompter technique for online therapy skills training. *Behavior Modification, 15*, 113–117.

Kruger, L. J., Cherniss, C., Maher, C., & Leichtman, H. (1988). Group supervision of paraprofessional counselors. *Professional Psychology, 19*, 609–616.

Ladany, N., Brittan-Powell, C. S., & Pannu, R. K. (1997). The influence of supervisory racial identity interaction and racial matching on the supervisory working alliance and supervisee multicultural competence. *Counselor Education and Supervision, 36*, 284–304.

Ladany, N., Constantine, M. G., Miller, K., Erickson, C. D., & Muse-Burke, J. L. (2000). Supervisor countertransference: A qualitative investigation into its identification and description. *Journal of Counseling Psychology, 47*, 102–115.

Ladany, N., & Friedlander, M. L. (1995). The relationship between the supervisory working alliance and trainees' experience of role conflict and role ambiguity. *Counselor Education and Supervision, 34*, 220–231.

Lanning, W. (1986). Development of the Supervisor Emphasis Rating Form. *Counselor Education and Supervision, 25*, 191–196, 207–209.

Lanning, W., & Freeman, B. (1994). The Supervisor Emphasis Rating Form—Revised. *Counselor Education and Supervision, 33*, 294–304.

Leary, T. (1957). *Interpersonal diagnosis of personality: A theory and a methodology for personality evaluation.* New York: Ronald Press.

Lehrman-Waterman, D., & Ladany, N. (2001). Development and validation of the Evaluation Process within Supervision Inventory. *Journal of Counseling Psychology, 48*, 168–177.

Leong, F. T. L., & Wagner, N. S. (1994). Cross-cultural counseling supervision: What do we know? What do we need to know? *Counselor Education and Supervision, 34*, 117–131.
Levenson, E. A. (1984). Follow the fox. In L. Caligor, P. M. Bromberg, & J. D. Meltzer (Eds.), *Clinical perspectives on the supervision of psychoanalysis and psychotherapy* (pp. 153–167). New York: Plenum.
Lewis, G. J., Greenburg, S. L., & Hatch, D. B. (1988). Peer consultation groups for psychologists in private practice: A national survey. *Professional Psychology, 19*, 81–86.
Liddle, B. J. (1986). Resistance in supervision: A response to perceived threat. *Counselor Education and Supervision, 26*, 117–127.
Liddle, H. A., & Schwartz, R. (1983). Live supervision/consultation: Conceptual and pragmatic guidelines for family therapy training. *Family Process, 22*, 477–490.
Linton, J. M. (2003). A preliminary qualitative investigation of group processes in group supervision: Perspectives of master's level practicum students. *Journal for Specialists in Group Work, 28*, 215–226.
Loevinger, J. (1976). *Ego development.* San Francisco, CA: Jossey-Bass.
Loganbill, C., Hardy, E., & Delworth, U. (1982). Supervision: A conceptual model. *The Counseling Psychologist, 10*(1), 3–42.
Maki, D. R., & Bernard, J. M. (2003). The ethics of clinical supervision. In R. R. Cottone & V. M. Tarvydas (Eds.), *Ethical and professional issues in counseling* (2nd ed.). Upper Saddle River, NJ: Prentice Hall.
Manzanares, M. G., O'Halloran, T. M., McCartney, T. J., Filer, R. D., Varhely, S. C., & Calhoun, K. (2004). CD-ROM technology for education and support of site supervisors. *Counselor Education and Supervision, 43*, 220–231.
Martin, J. S., Goodyear, R. K., & Newton, F. B. (1987). Clinical supervision: An intensive case study. *Professional Psychology, 18*, 225–235.
Martin, J., Slemon, A. G., Hiebert, B., Hallberg, E. T., & Cummings, A. L. (1989). Conceptualizations of novice and experienced counselors. *Journal of Counseling Psychology, 36*, 395–400.
Masters, M. A. (1992). The use of positive reframing in the context of supervision. *Journal of Counseling and Development, 70,* 387–390.
McCarthy, P., Sugden, S., Koker, M., Lamendola, F., Maurer, S., & Renninger, S. (1995). A practical guide to informed consent in clinical supervision. *Counselor Education and Supervision, 35*, 130–138.
McNeill, B. W., & Worthen, V. (1989). The parallel process in psychotherapy supervision. *Professional Psychology, 20*, 329–333.
Montalvo, B. (1973). Aspects of live supervision. *Family Process, 12*, 343–359.
Nelson, M. L., & Friedlander, M. L. (2001). A close look at conflictual supervisory relationships: The trainee's perspective. *Journal of Counseling Psychology, 48*, 384–395.
Nelson, M. L., & Holloway, E. L. (1990). Relation of gender to power and involvement in supervision. *Journal of Counseling Psychology, 37*, 473–481.
Nelson, M. L., & Holloway, E. L. (1999). Supervision and gender issues. In M. Carroll & E. L. Holloway (Eds.), *The practice of clinical supervision* (pp. 23–35). London: Sage.
Nelson, M. L., & Neufeldt, S. A. (1998). The pedagogy of counseling: A critical examination. *Counselor Education and Supervision, 38*, 70–88.
Neswald-McCalip, R. (2001). Development of the secure counselor: Case examples supporting Pistole & Watkins (1995) discussion of attachment theory in counseling supervision. *Counselor Education and Supervision, 48*, 18–27.

Neufeldt, S. A., Iversen, J. N., & Juntunen, C. L. (1995). *Supervision strategies for the first practicum.* Alexandria, VA: American Counseling Association.

Neufeldt, S. A., Karno, M. P., & Nelson, M. L. (1996). A qualitative study of experts' conceptualization of supervisee reflectivity. *Journal of Counseling Psychology, 43,* 3–9.

Osborn, C. J., & Davis, T. E. (1996). The supervision contract: Making it perfectly clear. *The Clinical Supervisor, 14*(2), 121–134.

Patterson, C. H. (1983). A client-centered approach to supervision. *The Counseling Psychologist, 11*(1), 21–25.

Pelling, N., & Renard, D. (1999). The use of videotaping within developmentally based supervision. *Journal of Technology in Counseling, 1*(1). Retrieved November 5, 2003, from http://jtc.colstate.edu/voll_l/supervision.htm

Penman, R. (1980). *Communication processes and relationships.* London: Academic Press.

Petty, R. E., & Cacioppo, J. T. (1986). *Communication and persuasion: Central and peripheral routes to attitude change.* New York: Springer-Verlag.

Piaget, J., & Inhelder, B. (1969). *The psychology of the child.* New York: Basic Books.

Pierce, R. M., & Schauble, P. G. (1970). Graduate training of facilitative counselors: The effects of individual supervision. *Journal of Counseling Psychology, 17,* 210–215.

Pierce, R. M., & Schauble, P. G. (1971). Toward the development of facilitative counselors: The effects of practicum instruction and individual supervision. *Counselor Education and Supervision, 11,* 83–89.

Pistole, M. C., & Watkins, C. E. (1995). Attachment theory, counseling process, and supervision. *The Counseling Psychologist, 23,* 457–478.

Presser, N. R., & Pfost, K. S. (1985). A format for individual psychotherapy session notes. *Professional Psychology, 16,* 11–16.

Remley, T. P., Jr., & Herlihy, B. (2001). *Ethical, legal, and professional issues in counseling.* Upper Saddle River, NJ: Prentice Hall.

Roberts, E. B., & Borders, L. D. (1994). Supervision of school counselors: Administrative, program, and counseling. *The School Counselor, 41,* 149–157.

Rogers, C. R. (1942). The use of electrically recorded interviews in improving psychotherapeutic techniques. *American Journal of Orthopsychiatry, 12,* 429–434.

Rønnestad, M. H., & Skovholt, T. M. (1993). Supervision of beginning and advanced graduate students of counseling and psychotherapy. *Journal of Counseling and Development, 71,* 396–405.

Rozsnafszky, J. (1979). Beyond schools of psychotherapy: Integrity and maturity in therapy and supervision. *Psychotherapy: Theory, Research and Practice, 16*(2), 190–198.

Schacht, A. J., Howe, H. E., & Berman, J. J. (1988). A short form of the Barrett-Lennard Inventory for supervisor relationships. *Psychological Reports, 63,* 699–703.

Schmidt, J. P. (1979). Psychotherapy supervision: A cognitive-behavioral model. *Professional Psychology, 10,* 278–284.

Schön, D. A. (1983). *The reflective practitioner: How professionals think in action.* New York: Basic Books.

Searles, H. F. (1955). The informational value of the supervisor's emotional experience. *Psychiatry, 18,* 135–146.

Sells, J. N., Goodyear, R. K., Lichtenberg, J. W., & Polkinghorne, D. E. (1997). Relationship of supervisor and trainee gender to in-session verbal behavior and ratings of trainee skills. *Journal of Counseling Psychology, 44*, 406–412.

Skovholt, T. M., & Jennings, L. (2004). *Master therapists: Exploring expertise in therapy and counseling*. Boston: Pearson.

Skovholt, T. M., & Rønnestad, M. H. (1992a). *The evolving professional self: Stages and themes in therapist and counselor development*. New York: Wiley.

Skovholt, T. M., & Rønnestad, M. H. (1992b). Themes in therapist and counselor development. *Journal of Counseling and Development, 70*, 505–515.

Skovholt, T. M., Rønnestad, M. H., & Jennings, L. (1997). In search of expertise in counseling, psychotherapy, and professional psychology. *Educational Psychology Review, <ill>* 361–369.

Stoltenberg, C. (1981). Approaching supervision from a developmental perspective: The counselor complexity model. *Journal of Counseling Psychology, 28*, 59–65.

Stoltenberg, C. D., & Delworth, U. (1987). *Supervising counselors and therapists: A developmental approach.* San Francisco: Jossey-Bass.

Stoltenberg, C. D., McNeill, B. W., & Crethar, H. C. (1994). Changes in supervision as counselors and therapists gain experience: A review. *Professional Psychology, 25*, 416–449.

Stoltenberg, C. D., McNeill, B. W., & Crethar, H. C. (1995). Persuasion and development in counselor supervision. *The Counseling Psychologist, 23*, 633–648.

Strong, S. R. (1968). Counseling: An interpersonal influence process. *Journal of Counseling Psychology, 15*, 215–224.

Strosahl, K., & Jacobson, N. S. (1986). Training and supervision of behavior therapists. *The Clinical Supervisor, 4*(1–2), 183–206.

Sumerel, M. B. (1994). Parallel process in supervision. In L. D. Borders (Ed.), *Supervision: Exploring the effective components* (ERIC Document Reproduction Service No. EDOCD-94–16). Greensboro, NC: ERIC/CASS.

Supervision Interest Network, Association for Counselor Education and Supervision. (1995). Ethical guidelines for counseling supervisors. *Counselor Education and Supervision, 34*, 270–276.

Sutton, J. M. (1997, January). *A descriptive study of the supervision of counselors as mandated by state statute and rule.* Paper presented at the annual meeting of the American Association of State Counseling Boards, Hot Springs, AR.

Tracey, T. J., Ellickson, J. L., & Sherry, P. (1989). Reactance in relation to different supervisory environments and counselor development. *Journal of Counseling Psychology, 36*, 336–344.

Warburton, J. R., Newberry, A., & Alexander, J. (1989). Women as therapists, trainees, and supervisors. In M. McGoldrick, C. Anderson, & F. Walsh (Eds.), *Women in families: A framework for family therapy* (pp. 152–165). New York: W. W. Norton.

Ward, L. G., Friedlander, M. L., Schoen, L. G., & Klein, J. G. (1985). Strategic self-presentation in supervision. *Journal of Counseling Psychology, 32*, 111–118.

Watkins, C. E. (1995). Pathological attachment styles in psychotherapy supervision. *Psychotherapy, 32*, 333–340.

Watson, J. C. (2003). Computer-based supervision: Implementing computer technology into the delivery of counseling supervision. *Journal of Technology in Counseling,*

3(1). Retrieved November, 5, 2003, from http://jtc.colstate.edu/vol3_1/Watson/Watson.htm

Werstlein, P. O., & Borders, L. D. (1997). Group process variables in group supervision. *Journal for Specialists in Group Work, 22*, 120–136.

Wessler, R. L., & Ellis, A. (1980). Supervision in rational-emotive therapy. In A. K. Hess (Ed.), *Psychotherapy supervision: Theory, research and practice* (pp. 181–191). New York: Wiley.

Whiston, S. C., & Emerson, S. (1989). Ethical implications for supervisors in counseling of trainees. *Counselor Education and Supervision, 28*, 318–325.

White, V. E., & Queener, J. (2003). Supervisor and supervisee attachments and social provisions related to the supervisory working alliance. *Counselor Education and Supervision, 42*, 203–218.

Wilbur, M. P., Roberts-Wilbur, J. M., Morris, J., Betz, R., & Hart, G. M. (1991). Structured group supervision: Theory into practice. *Journal for Specialists in Group Work, 16*, 91–100.

Worthington, E. L., Jr. (1984). Empirical investigation of supervision of counselors as they gain experience. *Journal of Counseling Psychology, 31*, 63–75.

Worthington, E. L., Jr. (1987). Changes in supervision as counselors and supervisors gain experience: A review. *Professional Psychology, 18*, 189–208.

Wright, L. M. (1986). An analysis of live supervision "phone-ins" in family therapy. *Journal of Marital and Family Therapy, 12*, 187–190.

Young, J. S., & Borders, L. D. (1998). The impact of metaphor on clinical hypothesis formation and perceived supervisor characteristics. *Counselor Education and Supervision, 37*, 238–256.

Young, J. S., & Borders, L. D. (1999). The intentional use of metaphor in counseling supervision. *The Clinical Supervisor, 18*(1), 139–149.

Name Index

Subject Index

S

T

V

W